FOXFIRE LIVING

FOXFIRE LIVING

DESIGN, RECIPES & STORIES
FROM THE MAGICAL INN IN THE CATSKILLS

ELIZA CLARK AND TIM TROJIAN

PHOTOGRAPHS BY ARDEN WRAY

HARPER DESIGN
An Imprint of HarperCollins Publishers

HarperCollins books may be purchased for educational, business, or sales promotional use. For information please email the Special Markets Department at SPsales@harpercollins.com.

Published in 2019 by
Harper Design
An Imprint of HarperCollins*Publishers*
195 Broadway
New York, NY 10007
Tel: (212) 207-7000
Fax: (855) 746-6023
harperdesign@harpercollins.com
www.hc.com

Distributed throughout the world by
HarperCollins*Publishers*
195 Broadway
New York, NY 10007

ISBN: 978-0-06-286323-2
Library of Congress Control Number: 2019026138

Design by Amanda Jane Jones
Printed in Canada
First Printing, 2019

The View from Here

I'M WRITING THIS from the edge of a cliff. I'm not even someone who really likes heights, and I definitely don't like the thought of falling. But sometimes in life, we're lured to the edge of a precipice because the splendor of a view beyond pulls us to stand at the teetering pinnacle and look out, gaze out as far as the eye can see, knowing that the view continues beyond that and beyond that and on, on, on. It's the brink. At some point, all dreamers end up there.

Since my husband, Tim, and I began to renovate Foxfire Mountain House two years ago, we have been living on the brink. Even the sound of it—*the brink*—conjures up a scary place, full of peril, spiked with obstacles and risk. And it is. We've honestly had more challenges and worries than we ever had in a lifetime leading up to this. But if you follow your heart and allow a dream to hope-walk you to the cliff's edge, what you find suddenly is that the air has a softness there, you are an eagle at the point of flight, and every brightest blue-sky possibility is within reach.

It's an understatement to say that the last two years of owning and operating Foxfire Mountain House have been a whirlwind. But it's actually the two years before when the wind started to pick up and the story truly begins. The story that is this book.

Back then, I was working as a television show-runner and Tim had recently left his gig as an executive chef and was debating what to do next. Like so many people we knew, we were caught up in a lifestyle of working crazy-long hours, not having any balance, and most importantly to us, not seeing each other enough. We were busy and tired and there didn't seem to be a way out of any of it. It was a life, but it wasn't the life we wanted. I was gone on the road most of the time working on various series, and we often said that the main thing we wanted for our lives was just to fall into bed together each night and wake up every morning in each other's arms. It seemed like such a simple thing to want to spend more time

with the person you love. But you know, it wasn't simple—it presented as a monolithic improbability. We had the usual bills and commitments and work ambition to achieve status in our fields. Then, on a moony August night, I came home late from a job and dropped my bags inside the front door. I made my way to the backyard to reconnect with Tim over a bottle of wine under the stars before I crashed into sleep, and I suggested we just . . . stop. Stop everything that we didn't want to do anymore.

I promise you, I startled myself as I said the words out loud. A hot current ran through me that I still remember, and I saw Tim nod in agreement with me. The electric frisson I felt was the instant acknowledgment that something dramatic had happened. It was done, and I understood it to my core. We were going to close the book on the life we'd been living as promptly as we could manage and start writing the pages of a brand-new book. A book that not a soul but us would, or could, write. All those pages were ours to fill. It was our story, our lives, to create.

We didn't have any savings, but we had a modest house with some equity that we could sell. We knew we wanted to embark on a project that we could do together, that would combine our skills and earn us a living, since we weren't ever likely to be in a position to retire. With our respective food and design passions, it was easy enough to settle on the plan to open a country inn with a restaurant that we would run together. While we'd never done this specific thing before, we could both *see* how to do it. Whether it was a kitchen or a television show, we had proven that we could both run a "show," a production, which is what any operation really is at its core. Opening a boutique hotel/country inn made sense to us. It made less sense to our friends and family, who cautioned us of the risks for what we were about to do—losing all our money, our relationship ending in a cruel divorce, terrible renovation accidents that we'd never recover

from—as if we weren't scared enough. Change is never easy, but the dream, and the fact that we are scrappy, optimistic, can-do, resourceful, gung ho, just-do-it, make-it-happen people, pulled us onward. We knew we had to dare to take the risk and try.

We decided to focus our hunt for a suitable property in the Catskill Mountains of New York for so many reasons, including the beauty of the natural surroundings (oh, birds, mushrooms, fly-fishing streams); the relative affordability of the real estate; and the proximity to New York City and Brooklyn, where we anticipated the majority of our hotel guests would come from. In our search, we found a real estate listing whose description was almost entirely for the little cottage on the property:

You'll be surprised by the open and airy contemporary interior with vaulted ceilings and artistic touches. Recently updated and freshly painted. Beautiful, level, and private 10 acres with spring-fed pond backed by NYS forest lands, and . . . BONUS: Vintage Hotel in pretty good condition considering its age.

When we first went to look at the rundown "bonus" hotel in the Catskills that is now Foxfire Mountain House, it was pouring rain and the grounds were a sea of mud. The building looked bleak and derelict. The roof had shingles missing, the porches were rotting and caving in. Inside, the guest rooms were scrawled with graffiti and painted all kinds of lurid colors, the floors were sloped, the windows had taped or missing glass. All in all, only the mice seemed at home. We were in and out of the place in five minutes—I felt that it was clearly way beyond the scope of our skills, so why waste time? It was definitely beyond our budget to fix a property as large and neglected as this one. But Tim had been quietly thoughtful as he walked through the three floors of the empty building, stopping to look out a window at the view of the mountains or knocking on walls to see if they were load-bearing. While I literally raced through ahead of him, careful not to touch anything because the dust was so thick and laced with cobwebs, and bolted out the back door boggled by the state of it all, Tim slowly trawled out behind me to our car, looking back over his shoulder at the old building as he got in. Our first impression wasn't exactly love at first sight.

We needed a place large enough for both guest rooms and a bar/restaurant, but all of the buildings we saw in our price range were in decrepit condition. We poked through a deteriorating ashram where the hole in the roof allowed rain to rather beautifully flow down a massive Buddha statue and rot out the floor underneath, as well as a couple of abandoned motor lodges. It sounds nutty, but we actually started to develop an eye for shabby, falling-in buildings. It takes some acclimatizing, but you can learn to look past the surface to the bones of a place. Tim's mantra became *Everything is fixable*. My mental response was always, *Sure, with enough money*. After we had toured several of these properties, Tim decided that he wanted to go back and look once more at the property that would become Foxfire.

This time, I viewed it with new eyes. Tim had been thinking about the property since we first looked at it and was quick to offer general restructurings of the layout, suggesting places where walls should be taken down and bathrooms joined to bedrooms. I spied lovely little details under the dust and an overall faded grandeur from the good-size rooms and multitude of windows. This was the first time that I saw Tim do something I've now seen so many times, a gesture that always makes me smile: He paced out the room we were in by placing one foot right in front of the other, heel to toe like a tightrope walker, to calculate the distance. His figuring is that his feet are each about twelve inches long and serve as a readily available measuring tape. (Tim also has measurements for the top knuckle of his thumb to the thumb tip—one inch; the width of his hand across the bottom knuckles with fingers together—four inches; his elbow to the tips of his fingers—eighteen inches . . . you get the idea. A measuring tape would be easier, but that is not Tim.) We met eyes as he turned and proclaimed that the kitchen could be enlarged by eight feet just by removing a wall that would be nothing at all to take down. He looked so delighted that honestly, if there had been a sledgehammer nearby, I think he would have shown me what he meant right then and there. That moment, watching Tim teeter across the room, as if on an invisible high wire, I fell in love all over again with him, and, too, with his optimism and creativity. Any risk was worth pursuing for the chance to wake up every day in each other's arms. I fell in love for the first time that moment with a hundred-plus-year-old hotel we were going to dare to save.

We both had average handyman skills, and I'd produced and directed home renovation series for television, but this was a huge project. We decided to do most of the work ourselves, since we couldn't afford to pay all the various trades to come in. For the first six months, we literally walked in circles trying to figure out where to start, how even to start. At first, we lived in the cottage because the real estate listing was right: it was quite nice and bright and airy. It had a fireplace in the living room and another one in the master bedroom, and all in all was a romantic place to be. It wasn't long, though, before we were needing to further fund the renovations, and so we listed the cottage on Airbnb, and Tim and I moved into a room on the second floor of the inn. We had no idea then that it would be four years until we had a private home of our own again.

We worried that at any moment we might go bust and the hotel renovation would get the better of us. We had limited skills and an even more limited budget. But we quickly learned to use what we had available, think outside the box, repurpose anything we could, and through it, a design philosophy—and a way of living—began to take shape.

We moved from one derelict room to another as we renovated the guest rooms on the second floor. It wasn't awful. At first, we had just an air mattress on the floor, a couple of lamps, and a stack of shelter magazines beside the bed that we could put a wine glass or coffee mug on depending on the time of day. While I thought of *The Shining* often the first year, especially running down the long dark hallway at night to the bathroom at the far end, Foxfire never felt creepy to either of us, even when it was at its most desolate.

A set of stairs from the main floor divides the second floor into two sides. We finished the two largest rooms and their bathrooms first so we could add those to our Airbnb rentals and bring in extra money while we continued to renovate. Tim came up with the rather ingenius idea of building a false wall

in the hallway so that behind it, the mess and chaos of renovations could be hidden, while in front, the rooms were decorated and ready to welcome guests. Tim erected the wall, and then we wallpapered it, hung a mirror on it, and placed an armchair and a wicker basket in front of it. Each time we finished a room, we moved the fake wall a bit farther down the hallway until eventually we could get rid of it all together. Later, more than once, return guests commented with wonderment that everything looked so much bigger with the renovations now complete! Many times over the two years it took to fully finish all the work, Tim and I had a sense of pride in the projects we'd done but also in the way we'd done them. Believe it, necessity is the mother of invention; Foxfire is living proof.

By our count, we've now hosted about fifteen thousand guests at Foxfire. Almost everyone asks us our story and wants to know how we did it: *Who did the design? What was the inspiration?* It's as if we are the front line of an experiment in daring to risk making a major life and career change and everyone wants to know if the experiment was successful. They look at us the way you'd examine some strange flora you found in the woods. Do we have more gray hairs, holes in our shoes, eye twitches? Did we really manage the whole project ourselves: selecting the paint colors, light fixtures, materials and furnishings, landscaping, the smallest details? Is it all . . . possible?

Foxfire Living is the story of those paint colors, light fixtures, materials, and furnishings. But it is also the story of how you can take your life into your own hands and create a personal narrative that reflects your truest desires. So many people are ready to stop and reevaluate, like we were. Since we began this journey, we can now honestly say that we crafted every one of the pages of our story. Tim and I fall asleep together every night, and we wake up together every morning by the beautiful inn that we created heel to toe, step by step. We look at Foxfire with so much love and amazement now. And here we are at the cliff's edge, still dazzled by the ever-unfolding view, our heads in the clouds, feet holding solid ground, ready for anything.

—*Eliza*

Foxfire's Field Rules

THIS BOOK IS a field guide to telling your home's story, inspired by the way a naturalist might jot down notes while wandering in the woods or observing the changing seasons or the waxing and waning of the moon. We figured out our design principles step by step through curiosity and trial and error. We kept track of our progress as we went along and have referenced these lessons often as we've jumped into other projects. We hope that this fieldwork will be useful to you in your own design journey.

Living in the Catskills, surrounded by so much beauty, has awakened us to the simple movement of each day, from the pale pink dawn to the rich indigo night sky blazing with silvery stars. The day's phases have been such an inspiration to our design journey, and so our design concepts unfold as the day unfolds—dawn, morning, day, dusk, night—which will allow you to move through each element of the design and renovation process in a natural and holistic way. A beautiful space is meant to be lived in, which includes life's daily needs and movements, so we've included recipes and DIY projects to give you the full experience of bringing Foxfire's magic into your own home, inspiring you to live your best life.

What you'll find is that at the heart of every design choice, recipe, and project in this book are these three principles that we call our field rules.

RESPECT WHAT'S THERE

We are always keenly aware of our setting, and it's important to take care not to destroy something's innate charm by making change for the sake of change. It's like if you had to describe a good friend's best traits to someone else—the design of a space starts with identifying the good traits and figuring out how to highlight them. And there's always something, even if it's initially hidden, like a wonderful view that's on the other side of a wall just waiting for a window to show it.

USE WHAT YOU HAVE

This concept is about thinking creatively and not being wasteful. We live by the rules of reusing and repurposing. Beams that we removed from the old veranda are now used on the ceiling of the lounge, for example. Sometimes it's as simple as seeing your current furniture in a new light and moving a piece into a different room for a quick refresh, or putting all your throw pillows in a pile and placing them in new spots throughout your space. It's not always about buying the next thing, but rather transforming an item you have into something else or using it in a different way to give it another life.

MAKE IT MAGIC

Finally, be original and pay thoughtful attention to all the details, from the planning through to the final result. Magic is the love child of care and creativity.

Throughout the book, you'll find echoes of these field rules in mini field notes, because we've kept them in mind from the start and continue to use them in every one of our design projects.

As Foxfire evolved and renovations continued, it became clear that the food we were developing

for our space was so entwined with design that our field rules applied to both. As soon as we pictured our guests waking up in a simple and serene bedroom tucked into linen sheets and snuggled under a soft throw, we pictured a hot cup of coffee and fresh biscuits at their bedside. Just as the bones of a room ("respect what's there") inspire the design, so too do the ingredients we find growing wild in our woods and fields, or farm fresh from the local market shelves, inspire the recipes. The process is organic and ever-evolving. We don't leave leftovers to take up space in the fridge indefinitely ("use what you have"). Meals are planned, sometimes daily, and the pantry is considered for the practicality and reuse of ingredients. Just as our restaurant menus are designed to incorporate overlapping ingredients both for ease and cost-effectiveness, the recipes offered here are designed for no waste at home. The result: We have suggested next-day menus for using up any leftover ingredients. Seasonal cooking is the best for this, since the products are fresh and ripe with a built-in life span that requires they be enjoyed promptly. Ingredients foraged and cooked over an open fire are ideal, and we do that often.

We are, at heart, ultimate do-it-yourselfers in every regard. For this book, there were just three of us who did everything: I decorated the spaces and did the writing, Tim did all of the cooking and recipe creation, and our daughter, Arden, did all the photography. We didn't have a crew, or any food and prop stylists, or even any special lighting equipment. The three of us figured it out as we went along, as we did with the design and conception of the inn. Anyone can do this. You just need to give yourself the freedom to play around, dive headlong into some explorations, try things out, and follow your intuition. It took us a minute to figure out that we needed to have the table settings ready for the dishes Tim was cooking before the food was finished or they'd sit too long and lose any steam or succulent drips before being

photographed. I have held up a white pillow as a light bounce for the camera more than once now. But we got there. Tim only insisted that we work within the parameters of the food being real "as cooked" and that we didn't fuss with it too much, no poking and prodding, no adding shining agents or colorings. Tim adores food so much that he has complete respect for its integrity, and to violate the food would be to wound his spirit. We all sat down and ate every single dish in this book after we photographed it. Each time, we had such a sense of excitement at being able to share with you everything that we'd been up to.

So this is our field guide to all that is Foxfire. It's who we are, how we are, how we do what we do, and how you can do it too. We hope you find it of use in your own creative wanderings as you design your best life. **o**

Writing Your Home's Story

WE'RE ASKED OFTEN if we have a signature style at Foxfire, and I would say it's rustic simplicity, both in the food and the decor. We like simple, unfussy natural materials that age well and are somehow honest and approachable. Signs that an object has been loved and lived with—a little tarnish on old brass, faded and time-worn leather, or an oil painting with the canvas frayed at the edges—only adds to an object's beauty. Textures are the key to creating spaces with soul, and we love linens, leather, wood, stone, silk, wool, steel, ceramics, plaster. Marrying rough with smooth works so well (think of a velvet chair against a stone wall). Opposites do attract. At times, we've called our style rustic glam and rough lux, but labels are hard, and different spaces call for different design treatments.

So where do you start when you're writing your own home's design story? The two main questions I ask when I am about to design a room are *How will the space be used?* (which helps decide what flooring, furniture, and lighting it will need) and *What's the desired mood for the space?* (the mood can be called other things like "style" or "vibe," and it determines how you'll feel in the space). Basically, it comes down to deciding how you want the space to function and how you want to feel when you're in it, and that's generally a reliable starting point for any room's design. But Foxfire wasn't like that.

Foxfire was built in the early 1900s and opened as a hotel in 1914. It's about 7,500 square feet with eleven guest rooms, a long veranda with columns that faces a garden courtyard, a lounge with a fireplace, and a restaurant bar. There is also a three-bedroom cottage adjacent to the hotel. The building is made of wood clapboard and has a

lovely belfry on top. It looks like a classic Catskills summer resort. It's set on ten private acres with a pond, lily pool, and forest and is backed by mountains with forever-wild New York State land. It used to be called Mountain Breeze House (opposite) and women and children would spend the whole summer at the inn while the men would venture upstate every Friday on "the husband train" and go back on Sundays to work in New York City for the week. The motto then was "Your home away from home!"

By the time we encountered it, the building was too big, too complicated, and it needed so much work that we didn't really know how to answer even those basic questions. The main-floor lounge could have sofas and chairs, *or* it could have a cocktail bar and dining tables. Did we want our guests to have dinner in front of the fire, or drinks while they played a board game, or to snuggle on a sofa? Tim had ideas, and I had ideas, but neither of us was certain yet what we wanted our guests to do in the space or how we wanted them to feel. Should we go mid-century modern or granny chic or rustic farmhouse or Scandinavian? We were overwhelmed by the scope of the whole project and the underlying pressure. A nagging voice in the back of our minds told us if we made a mistake with the design, this would be an uncomfortable, unattractive, unpopular, wildly unsuccessful place that nobody would want to come visit and we'd never make a living and that would be a wrap, folks, on our grand adventure.

Faced with the enormity of the undertaking, Tim poured us each a glass of wine in front of the fire. We had to figure out a plan for how to start getting stuff done. We decided to take a step back and

CATSKILL **FIELD NOTE** MOUNTAINS

CREATING YOUR CHARACTER

Here are a few basic questions to help you begin creating a character to start your design story.

1) Who lives here?
2) What do they do?
3) What are their passions, hobbies, favorite pastimes?
4) How would they like to use the space?
5) What features will make the space function best for the way they want to use it?

pretend this wasn't our place but someone else's. Essentially by chance, and through sheer desperation, we came up with an imagination game, a creative exercise that helped us write the story of the house.

It started with a simple question that gave us the distance and objectivity to consider the space free of our own personal quandaries. *Who owns this house?* Tim posed the question, and it hung between us for just a few seconds because, remarkably, I could answer it. I saw immediately what Tim meant: The owner of this house was a person who loved everything I loved. I could describe him, because in a far-off, dreamy, mind's-eye way, I could see him. Tim and I rapid-fired thoughts to each other: the "owner's" traits, habits, passions, and tastes. Out of thin air, "Uncle Desmond" came to life. Creating this fictional character helped us to define our own style and visualize clearly the overall look and vibe we wanted, and how the elements might come together to form the substance of an actual design plan. It took the pressure off us feeling like we could make a costly mistake and allowed us just to play.

From these initial traits, we could further define Uncle Desmond. He likes a whiskey at night by the fire. He prizes sleeping well and getting up early to make coffee and go for a hike. Simple pleasures make his day. Uncle Desmond became very real to us. So much so, that when we came across a small oil portrait hanging in an antiques store (opposite), we recognized him instantly. We look at the painting often and as fondly as a true relative.

Perhaps this all sounds peculiar, but it worked for us as a method that we now rely on for every renovation and decorating project we do. The design choices stem from the personality outline. So much of creating a space, or even deciding what outfit you want to wear on any given day, is about creating a persona, for instance: *Today I'm going to a business meeting, so I'll wear a power suit but I want to present as creative and current, so it'll be a velvet suit, and I'll wear my hair in a messy ponytail.*

Based on how we perceived Uncle Desmond, we knew that we should keep the bones of the space simple but bring in depth and personality with the accessories. The majority of the walls at Foxfire

are painted a warm white. Vintage lighting and furnishings are one-of-a-kind, beautifully made, and most of all, comfortable. Foxfire has collections of butterflies, moths, antlers, and shells. In fact, even the name Foxfire came from our deep-dive into Uncle Desmond's personality. We wanted a name that was evocative of the natural world, but it wasn't until we pictured Uncle Desmond exploring in the damp woods, writing his field notes to chart his observations and findings, that we thought of the word *foxfire*: a bioluminescent fungus that causes decaying wood to have a soft bluish-green glow. Sometimes called fairy light or will-o'-the-wisp, this natural phenomenon is mysterious and other-worldly, but in folklore is said to have burned bright enough at times to lead weary travelers home.

Like Uncle Desmond, we scribbled our own field notes as we wandered our way through designing Foxfire from the ground up: observations, design tricks we learned the hard way and didn't want to forget, scrawled projects, and recipe thoughts. It's been a long and winding road, full of mishaps and missteps, joy and pride, blood (yes), tears (yes), sweat (yes), and the journey continues. ◦

UNCLE DESMOND TURNER

He's eccentric and worldly, the rich uncle you've only heard about who looks like he lives in the 1930s. He's a gentleman and a rogue, a scholar and naturalist, an adventurer. Athletic, extroverted, curious, modern. A wanderer who has explored all corners of the globe collecting artifacts, antiques, trophies, and wonders of the natural world. He has fine tastes but not in the usual sense of flaunting his wealth and privilege, so his possessions are not showy but are of quality. He appreciates comfort and the patina of age. He prefers worn velvet and leather for his furniture; old silver, pewter, and brass over the flash of new copper; interesting art and music. He believes in bringing nature indoors in all ways because the world is glorious: moths, butterflies, hornets' and birds' nests, shells, bones, fungi, lichen, exotic plants. He is rooted in the Catskills but spices his food and his rooms with flavors that recall the far-off places of his travels.

CHAPTER ONE

DAWN

OBSERVATION.   IDENTIFICATION.   DISCOVERY.

I'VE ALWAYS LOVED nature and studying bugs and leaves and feathers and shells. When you really stop to examine something, there's a shift that takes place where your focus moves from the macro to the micro. A green leaf, when studied, reveals its rivers of veins and tiny holes; an ordinary shell is discovered to have gently swirling chambers and a pale opalescence not suspected from the gray outer housing. Designing a room or cooking a meal can be viewed in the same way: you begin with the macro and then narrow down to the micro. When setting out to design a space, your first objective is to see and study the big picture of what you have, the bones of your space, before you finesse the details.

In our world, we are lucky that Tim just instinctively has a macro way of seeing things and I have micro vision, so our individual strengths complement each other well. (When we agree, that is.) I'll admit that I'm not always the best at figuring out where walls could come down or where to add extra windows or doorways to make the most of a space, but I've found that the best way to figure this out is by imagining your dream space over what's actually in front of you. Do you want more natural light, or a better flow between rooms for convenience or to facilitate tasks that will be done in that space? For example, if more natural light is needed, is it possible to add another window to the outside? If not, then what about an interior window on an inside wall or French doors that allow light to filter in from an adjoining room? The same can be said for flow. Would it be easier to move straight from the kitchen into the dining room when entertaining? Or a bedroom into a bathroom? If so, can you take down a wall or open one up? I think this is why you see homeowners who choose to live in a space for a while before they jump into renovating, because the routines of daily life make it abundantly clear what's working and what isn't with the spaces. In our case, we didn't have that luxury, so we just had to rely on Tim's good macro vision and my micro way of enhancing what's already in place to get to the heart of what big renovations we needed to do to make the spaces functional for us and our guests. We realized early on that the renovation process, both inside and out, would require a lot of compromising as we each tried to settle on the best design choices out of the zillions we tossed around. ○

Looking Past the Surface

THRIFTINESS, A DESIRE to preserve a space's charm by highlighting and enhancing its natural attributes, and doing so with originality, were all spurs to our creativity when coming up with our design plans. The first design lesson we learned was teaching ourselves to see past what was present at face value and instead focus on the raw form of a space with the goal of transforming it either by physically changing it or by seeing it differently enough to work a refreshing overhaul. The same is true for the items that would fill the rooms. We kept an open mind when shopping, often digging through antiques barns and salvage yards to find items we liked the shape of that we could make into something useful or repurpose to be used in a different way. We're magpies. Always, our first go-to is to see if we can reuse something we already have on hand or transform it. We're not hoarders or overly "crafty," so the process can be fast, just a quick query to ourselves. For instance, before throwing out an old door, we'll ponder if we can use it anywhere else or turn it into something new, like a headboard or a dining table. As a culture, we all need to shift from thinking so much is disposable. I've produced and directed renovation shows, and we watch them on TV, and they almost all start with demo day where walls get torn down and cabinetry is ripped out with dramatic vigor. Personally, we take more care with demo. Often, cabinets and countertops can be salvaged and donated to local charities like Habitat for Humanity's ReStore so they don't end up as more landfill.

We had so many rooms to make over at Foxfire that we needed to be practical and budget-conscious, and that inspired us to get creative. An empty room can be daunting, but it's the best way to study its bones: the height of the ceiling; the number of windows; the position of the doorways; the sources of light—what's good and what's lacking. From my years in television when we would show "before" and "after" shots of renovated rooms, I can offer this tip: take photos of the room you're working on from each of the four corners. It's so much easier to get a sense of the scale and structure from the picture and to figure out the best furniture placement.

Once we began focusing on the structure, we couldn't help but start to see patterns for what worked and would make our lives easier in terms of cost and labor. Early on, we agreed that if one of us was adamant about a design choice, if that person ever pulled out the "this really matters to me" card, then the other one would give in. It was mutually understood that you couldn't use the card often, so it would retain its value and importance. It seemed like a fair plan until the day that we both used the "it really matters to me" card at the same time.

Originally, the front of the hotel was built with two large dormer windows on the third

---

(opposite) To be sure, the tub room is slightly weird-looking, or at the very least, unique-looking. I can personally attest, though, to the glory of soaking there in all four seasons, whether with the window wide open to the breeze in summer or with snowflakes softly drifting down in winter. The spa tub instantly became a guest favorite and a coveted spot to unwind during stays, as well as a popular Instagram pic to post for the novelty of it. Go, Tim.

floor, but at some time along the way, a narrower dormer had been tacked on to accommodate a rickety fire escape ladder that exited out a short door at the end of the dormer onto the veranda roof. This narrow dormer spoiled the symmetry, throwing off the overall balance of the exterior appearance. To me, there was no question that it took away from the architectural integrity of the historic building and I wanted pretty desperately to remove it, so I pulled out the card: "This really matters to me." Because I'm normally someone who likes to preserve what's there and make it work, this was a big deal.

Tim, on the other hand, didn't want to rip the dormer out and get rid of it. Not only would that be expensive, it would mean losing potentially valuable interior space. Renos generally are all about adding space, not taking it away, so it went against the grain for him. So, as he does, Tim started pitching ideas to me. Various possibilities for how the narrow dormer could be repurposed and even look good. My reaction to all the suggestions was: "Meh."

But then he hit on it. We had already decided the third-floor guest rooms would need to share bathrooms in the classic boardinghouse style of the old Catskills based on the way the building was structured—five queen guest rooms would share two bathrooms. It meant that those rooms could be slightly lower priced for guests compared to the rooms with en suite bathrooms, so overall we could appeal to travelers with different-size budgets. But, Tim suggested, what if we could change the layout to be *three* shared bathrooms among the five rooms instead of two—that would be better, right? There was no arguing with the logic, of course. Tim proposed making one of the bathrooms larger than we were going to and splitting it into two self-contained halves. One side would contain just a toilet and sink, and the other side would incorporate the narrow dormer and be a stand-alone shower with a soaking tub. A true *bath*room. Tim had done the measurements, and a deep spa-like soaking tub would fit very precisely into the dormer space with no real construction

needed. A lovely new window could replace the old door to the fire escape that would be at the foot of the tub and enable a beautiful treetop view with the peak of Mount Tremper beyond. ○

(opposite and below) Figuring out the dormer and third-floor bathroom situation was as hard as deciding what to do with the lounge fireplace was easy. When we first bought the building, the fireplace stood in the center of the room and was boxed in with drywall. A simple, homemade wooden mantel framed the brick hearth, but there was a teasing row of stones visible inside the frame, hinting that a rustic stone fireplace had once existed. There was no doubt in either of our minds that the natural stones must have been covered up for a reason, and that a crumbling mess of ruined mortar and missing rocks lay beneath. But we had a wanton moment when we decided we had nothing to lose since the current drywall situation would need to be changed anyway. After some hammering and prying, the most beautiful handmade floor-to-ceiling river-stone fireplace was revealed. Not a thing wrong with it! And it remains the only good thing we ever found behind the walls of Foxfire. (You don't even want to know.)

(above) In the same way that we taught ourselves to look past the surface traits to really focus on the bones of the space, this approach was also helpful when shopping for furniture and accessories (almost always vintage). We put aside our feelings about ugly finishes or a piece's intended function and instead looked at the actual shape of it and used our imaginations to think about how it could be restyled or repurposed. A great example of this is the pendant lights over the table in the dining room alcove which are a pair of old glass lamp bases that have been stripped of any fittings. Although they were not intended for this purpose, they are a fabulous shape and color (and only $40 for the pair). We ran cord and bulb kits through the pieces of two black candlesticks from Target and voilà, bespoke pendant lights for super cheap.

(opposite) We made the copper light fixture in the lobby from old lamp parts we found at our local weekend flea market. We dug through two dirty cardboard boxes piled with pieces of lamp parts, pulling out bits with a good bronze patina or filigree in the metal. We puzzled the pieces out on the grass of the stall until the shape of something like an actual light fixture was fashioned. Then we scurried back to Foxfire with a quasi plan for all the pieces and assembled it. We probably spent $15 total.

(opposite) In the first months as new owners of Foxfire, a lot of our time was spent
clearing out random stuff left behind by the previous owners. We filled and emptied and
refilled at least five huge dumpsters with junk and debris. We gave everything a hard
look to see if it could be saved and reused. We discovered a big triangular-shaped steel
something or other abandoned in the woods that we were about to toss in the dumpster
when Tim decided it actually looked kind of cool. To this day, we still don't know what it
is (maybe you will) but we built a wood stand for it and a roof and it's fully functional as
one of our wood sheds.

Make a Plan,
Use What You Have

WE HAD A can-do approach with Foxfire because we had no choice about it in terms of our budget limitations for the size of the renovation we were doing. We weren't jumping to tile walls or sew curtains or paint every surface of everything, but we're glad now it was that way. Nothing is overly hard to do. It's really not. For sure, you want to prepare for a task by doing good research in advance. But from there, you pretty much just roll up your sleeves and get to it. Just dive in, and if you make a mistake, then improvise and no doubt you'll still come up with something better than the way it used to be. The more fully do-it-yourself we became, the more willing we were to try just about anything.

So many of our design elements began with one of us doing a scribbled drawing on a napkin at our local bar or on the back of an envelope from the day's mail while we sipped our morning coffee. Such was the case for the wall we erected in the dining room to block out more space behind it for a larger kitchen. The wall started out as a wall. Then, Tim smoothed the square napkin his beer had been on and drew a window in the wall so that you could see into the working kitchen from the dining room, which could also serve as a pass-through—beauty and function. I spun the napkin around to face me and added a rectangle below the window to make a niche. Then Tim added tiles to the wall. So there was the plan.

Tim tiled the right side of the wall while I tiled the left side. We polished off a bottle of bubbly as we went, and it was actually fun chatting and setting the tiles. The only thing was, the next morning Tim had to pry off my top three rows of tiles and redo them because they all sloped away on an

angle thanks to the champagne. *Wabi sabi*, right?

Tiling mistakes can be somewhat easily corrected, but other DIY projects are more daunting when it comes to learning as you go.

We decided to make a concrete bar in the dining room as a trial by fire. We knew it would weigh a ton, and since the wood floor had no subfloor below it for added support, we belly-crawled under the inn to pour footings for six-by-six timbers that would go directly into the ground to hold the bar's weight. We designed the shape that was a classic *L* with a sunken trough for bar condiments, built a frame mold, added steel mesh, hand mixed the concrete, and poured it in place. We covered the whole thing in plastic to keep it damp while it set. So far so good.

The problem came with our timing. The first problem, that is. This was mid-February in the Catskills during a cold snap. In order to set, the concrete had to stay above 50 degrees Fahrenheit, and with all the drafty old windows in the dining room, we had a hard time keeping the room warm enough. We brought in blower heaters and turned them up full blast. We needed to regularly spritz the concrete as it set, which meant twenty-four-hour vigilance for about a week. That all was an effort but went fine until it was time to finish the bar with a good sanding.

The concrete bar top (page 40) had to be smoothed and polished with a diamond wet grinder. Have you ever tried to give a big shaggy dog a bath when they're not inclined to have a bath? Multiply that amount of water flying around by a billion with a wet grinder. We had to essentially create a plastic room around the bar,

covering the ceiling, walls, and floor. We hooked a hose to a sink that was fifty feet away, and while one person used the grinder, the other tried to shop-vac up the spouting water. The grinder has to be kept pressed flat against the surface as it sands or it will gouge chunks out of the concrete. We also discovered that we'd made the condiments trough about a quarter inch smaller than the size of the grinder, so we had to laboriously hand sand that entire section. To sum up, you definitely get soaked, everything gets soaked, but then you have an amazing polished concrete bar that you can sit and have a glass of champagne at any time you want forever more. We upholstered the front of the bar with indigo kilim rugs for a pop of color and texture. ○

CATSKILL · FIELD NOTE · MOUNTAINS

LEARN FROM OUR MISTAKES

1) Quotes from outside contractors never actually reflect the final price. In our experience, the price will often almost double from what it seemed like it would be in the beginning. Some unexpected issue will always arise that adds to the overall cost. Budget for double the quote up front so you're not scrambling later, as we were many times.

2) Figure out when sales are happening for your key items and work with that timing. We bought all the paint for the hotel two weeks before our local paint store held their twice-yearly 40 percent off sale, costing us hundreds of dollars more than we needed to spend. Carpet and flooring often goes on sale before the holidays. Check if a sale is coming before you buy, or take advantage of a sale if you find a good one.

3) Curtain panels may list their length as, say, 96 inches on the packaging, and so you'll go ahead and measure that length from the floor, drill holes into the wall, and mount the curtain rod only to find they're actually not at all the length they say they are. One panel may be 95 inches and the other may be 94.5 inches, but neither is truly 96 inches, which is the height of your newly installed curtain rod. Measure the actual panels first, *then* hang the rod.

4) If you've made a placement mistake with your anchors, just hammer them deeper into the wall, spackle the hole, and paint. Don't use pliers to remove them, as you'll end up with a massive hole that pretty much is always visible no matter what you do.

5) Don't listen to no, especially where vintage materials are concerned. Contractors never want to bother with fitting beautiful old doorknobs or amazing unpolished brass faucets. They want you to grab something generic from a big-box store so they don't have to figure out how to make your old, exquisite (and nonstandard) item work. We've given in more than once and then been sad and envious to see so many beautiful pictures online from other homeowners who figured out how to get the old pieces to work. There's always a way.

Making a Vintage Daybed

DAYBEDS ARE KIND of amazing. More than a couch but less than an actual bed, they promote lounging and napping, alone or piled with friends for a movie night. At Foxfire, we made a daybed for the glass house where we hold cocktail parties. It's perfect for groups because it acts as a two-sided sofa where guests can sit back to back. Flea markets and thrift stores often have nice old spindle headboards for sale that are perfect for repurposing into a custom daybed. Be mindful of their size when shopping though, since three-quarter beds (a size between twin and a full or double bed) used to be popular, but mattresses for this size bed are often more expensive. We recommend purchasing twin-sized headboards for the most cost-effective mattress options. Take a measuring tape along and check that the headboard is about 38 inches wide to make life easy. It wouldn't be like us to make our own lives easy though, especially when we came across these great headboards with a Moroccan vibe, so our daybed has three-quarter headboards and a twin mattress—we just live with the extra space on either side, and it's really not that noticeable. Daybeds look their bohemian best with a jumble of inviting, cushy pillows.

YOU'LL NEED

- Two vintage twin-size headboards

- 1 twin-size mattress

- Tape measure

- 2 1-inch x 6-inch clear pine boards cut to the length of the mattress plus one inch (usually 76 inches), for side rails

- 2 2-inch x 6-inch pine boards cut to the length of the mattress plus one inch (usually 76 inches), for support beams

- 8 4-inch wood screws

- Drill with drill bits

- Sandpaper (optional)

- Wood stain or paint of your choosing

- 25 yards 4-inch-wide burlap webbing

- Staple gun and staples

1. Find a pair of vintage wood twin-sized headboards at a thrift shop. It's best to use two headboards, rather than a headboard and footboard, to keep it from looking too much like an actual bed.

2. Measure your mattress; most twin mattresses are 38 x 75 inches. Measure and mark the width of the mattress plus one inch on each side on each of the headboards. Then, mark four spots on each headboard using this width as a guide: bottom left corner 2 inches up from the bottom, bottom left corner 4 inches up from the bottom, bottom right corner 2 inches up from the bottom, bottom right corner 4 inches up from the bottom. Pre-drill holes in each of the 8 marked spots.

3. Mark two spots at each 1 x 6-inch clear pine board end to correspond with the holes in the headboards. Use a drill to attach the boards to the pre-drilled spots on the headboards with 4-inch wood screws. We used black wood screws that look good even if they show.

4. Next, screw in the two 2 x 6-inch pine boards at even intervals in between the outside rails, about 12 inches apart. These will function as the support beams for the mattress.

5. Stain or paint the headboards and side rails so that they match, sanding first, if necessary. We used a dark brown, almost black stain for ours. Let dry completely.

6. Starting under the inside of the side rail right next to the headboard, fold the end of the burlap webbing under about a half an inch for a tidy finish, then staple it to the inside of the wood beam to secure it. Then, run it up over the front face of the side rail, across the middle support beams (stapling the webbing to these beams for extra hold), then around the outside of the far side rail and up underneath to the other side. Fold the webbing under about a half inch for a tidy finish on the other side, and staple in place on the inside of the beam. Continue attaching strips of webbing at about 1-inch intervals until you reach the opposite headboard. This will act as a support for the mattress. We ended there for simplicity, but if you like, you can also nail decorative wood or upholstery tacks to the face of the burlap straps for a more finished look.

7. Add on your mattress and finish the look with a pretty covering and a ton of pillows.

Renovating from the Inside Out

AT THE SAME time that we were renovating inside, we were also creating gardens and landscaping outside. Gardens have to be one of the clearest examples of a labor of love. You plant and weed and mulch and prune, and most of all you wait for the plants to grow into their full glory. The property is surrounded by forest but had almost no ornamental plantings. We regularly watch gardening shows on TV, and we always roll our eyes at the ease with which holes are dug and new plants tamped ever so gently and effortlessly into the soft ground. If you dust aside the soil at Foxfire, lying in malevolent wait beneath the surface are a whole lot of rocks. Digging a simple hole is a backbreaking, joyless task that often involves a pickax, then a wheelbarrow to cart the heavy rocks away. We enlisted the help of friends and paid local workers with strong backs to jump in and work with us. Foxfire was growing quickly into a project that would need more hands on deck than just Tim and me plugging away if it was ever to get finished.

The long front veranda faces what is now a courtyard in front of a steeply sloped forested hillside. When we bought Foxfire, the whole area was just mud and debris. We knew we wanted to create a serene garden in that space for guests to look at when they were being served dinner outside or were lounging on the veranda. Since it's surrounded by tall trees, we chose plants that were hardy, shade-tolerant, and had pale flowers. White or light flowers are the best for when a garden will most often be enjoyed after dark, since the flowers can still be seen, whereas colored flowers blur into the night.

Probably the biggest outdoor decision we had to make was what to do with the abandoned swimming pool on the property. It had been partially destroyed and caved in at one end and many of the original patterned tiles had come off and been lost. We just didn't have the money or the time to rebuild a new pool, so we initially thought we would fill it in and get rid of it. But it was such a pretty shape, and the pavers around it leading to the glass house made a nice walkway, so we started playing with ideas for what it could be. Everything we came up with was going to be too expensive.

The bottom of the pool had already partially filled in with dirt and rainwater and had cattails growing along one side. Tim floated the idea of letting it fully naturalize. Cheap and brilliant! We used rocks dug up from the garden to fill in the side of the pool that had been destroyed so it now looked intentional. Tim rigged a recirculating pump to sit between the rocks that would create a small waterfall over the edge. We planted irises, grasses, and marsh plants along the "shore" of wet dirt that sloped into the pool and then added some water lilies in the center of the pool where it was deepest. During the day, the lily pool is serenely stunning, as the gorgeous pink and white lily flowers lavishly sprawl open to the sun between the lush green and maroon leaf pads. As the sun drifts down behind the mountain, the lilies close their petals inward and the frog songs swell, rising louder with the lift of the moon and the night sky glistening with stars. ○

The simple, natural beauty of the Catskills was a constant inspiration for both our indoor and outdoor designs, so we knew we wanted our own gardens to keep some of that same loose wildness. We used what was growing naturally on the grounds, shaped it, and added thoughtfully chosen plantings for their hardiness, color, and deer resistance to make it all flow together.

We plotted out a kitchen garden to grow herbs and vegetables that we can pick for fresh use in the restaurant. We mixed in raised wicker garden beds so we can change and control the soil depending on the plants we're growing, like lavender that likes well-drained, sandy soil.

(opposite) For structure and height in the courtyard garden, we built a gnarly wood arbor with a thatched roof so that the ground stays dry underneath. We add flowers and vines to the arbor in the summer months, and evergreen boughs to it throughout the winter. To me, it's become even more beautiful with a growth of common tree fungus that adds texture and color.

(above left and right) Other tucked-away spots that visitors can discover are a hammock nestled between two trees and a vintage pair of concrete shell chairs in the woods overlooking the stream.

(left) We added a concrete fountain as a focal point, leaving the water still since I personally don't like the sound of constant running water. We encouraged moss to grow on the fountain so it would blend in with the greenery and become part of the surroundings rather than standing out as too bright or new. We often float candles and flowers in the fountain, and it's a really lovely feature. We always wanted to have secret magical places to discover all around Foxfire, and the fountain is one of those places.

DAWN

RECEIPES

OUR DESIGN PHILOSOPHIES that encompass Foxfire's field rules—respect what's there, use what you
have, and make it magic—carry over brilliantly into
our kitchen's recipes. As much as possible, we use
ingredients that either grow wild on the property
and can be foraged, like thyme and ramps, or that
we plant in our gardens, like cardoons and mint.
Locally, Catskill mountain streams run with trout,
and we're connected to nearby farm producers for
our meats. Tim has created the recipes throughout
the book and written the introductions to them,
so you'll hear his voice too, learn some of his
history, and, I believe, sense his passion. I've been
lucky enough to watch him at work in the kitchen
so often, in his element, fully engaged, creating,
tasting, and all the while, whether he's even
completely aware of it or not, making magic to
share with the rest of us.

Fire-Cooked Quinoa and Dried Fruits Cereal

SERVES 6

I'M **OFTEN OUT** of bed and cooking before anyone else wakes up. I go to the kitchen when it's dark outside, and sometimes I don't leave until it's dark outside again. As one of the owners of Foxfire, as well as the only chef in the early days, I quickly established a morning ritual that involved gathering the ingredients for this hearty breakfast cereal, brewing a pot of coffee, then heading to the lounge to start the fire. The embers from the night before would usually still be glowing, so the fire would spark quickly and take the chill out of the room. This warm and satisfying breakfast dish that I make in a cast-iron pot over the open flames of the fireplace emphasizes these cozy, early-morning feelings. I wanted to develop a dish that anyone could enjoy, so this is vegan, gluten-free, dairy-free, and nut-free, which are the most common dietary restrictions we encounter at Foxfire. It's easily made from ingredients that are on hand in the pantry, and to me it's delicious.

1. Rinse the quinoa well.

2. Place the quinoa, water, and the remaining ingredients in a heavy-bottomed pot.

3. Bring the pot to a boil over an open fire or on the stove over high heat. Move the pot from the direct flames once it gets going, or reduce the heat to medium low.

4. Stir occasionally; the fruit can stick to the bottom and burn if you totally ignore it, which can happen if: you get busy making other dishes, chopping more wood, or watching the wild birds at the feeders. (Speaking from experience.)

5. Let simmer until the grain is soft and the water is absorbed. This dish can be served like any hot breakfast cereal: on the drier side or super moist, based on your preference.

USE WHAT YOU HAVE 1) Extra quinoa is easy to reuse in a tabbouleh or tossed in with a salad to impart a nutty taste and add protein. **2)** Consider tossing extra sunflower or pepita seeds into a risotto, salad, or on top of other breakfast cereals.

1½ cups (255 g) white quinoa

3¼ cups (813 ml) water (The dried fruit will absorb some of the water so a little extra is needed.)

¼ cup (35 g) each golden raisins, currants, and dried cranberries (You can easily substitute any dried fruit you have, or prefer. I sometimes switch it up with diced apricots or pears.)

¼ cup (35 g) hulled pepita seeds, unsalted

¼ cup (35 g) hulled sunflower seeds, unsalted

1 teaspoon salt

Wild Thyme and Cheddar Biscuits

**MAKES
12 BISCUITS**

I WAS BORN in New Orleans and moved around the South as a kid since my father was a pastor. For this reason, hot, freshly made biscuits are a breakfast staple to me. I developed this recipe for biscuits that are easy to make and consistently good, with the least fuss and mess possible. The dry mixture can be stored in the freezer in a plastic bag, ready for instant use any morning. I've found the trick to a drop biscuit is to get layers in the dough while keeping it in the bowl without overworking it. Because flour will have different moisture levels depending on how it was stored, the time of year, and where you are in the world, there is no exact measure for the buttermilk. You just have to eyeball it to get the dough to hold together.

4 cups (500 g) all-purpose flour, plus 1 cup (125 g) extra for dusting

3 teaspoons baking powder

2 teaspoons salt

1 teaspoon baking soda

⅞ cup (396 g) very cold unsalted butter, diced into ½-inch chunks

⅓ cup (42 g) grated white sharp cheddar cheese

¼ cup stripped whole thyme leaves

Approximately 1 cup (250 ml) buttermilk

2 eggs, beaten

Coarse sea salt

1. Preheat the oven to 400°F (204°C) and line a baking sheet with parchment paper. Set aside.

2. Add the flour, baking powder, salt, and baking soda to the bowl of a food processor.

3. Hold the pulse button and drop the butter chunks in piece by piece. Pulse until the butter is just chopped into the flour mixture. It should resemble coarse sand—do not over process.

4. Pour the mixture into a cold mixing bowl. (The main idea behind a biscuit is to keep the butter as cold as possible so the flour coats the tiny pieces.)

5. Add the cheddar cheese and thyme, and then pour about ½ cup of the buttermilk into the mix and fold together. Keep adding buttermilk until the mixture just holds together and forms a ball. If you added a little too much buttermilk, add some flour to tighten the mix back up.

6. Once the mix is ready, sprinkle some flour over the ball and fold the ball in half. Repeat three more times to create layers.

7. With an ice cream scoop or a large spoon, scoop out the mixture and place on the parchment-lined baking sheet.

8. Brush the top of the biscuits with the beaten eggs and sprinkle with coarse sea salt.

9. Bake until golden brown, about 20 minutes.

USE WHAT YOU HAVE If there are extra biscuits left, turn them into a savory parson's pudding, a dish that's much like a bread pudding but with biscuits in place of bread. Add the usual eggs and milk, a bit more of the cheddar cheese, and some ham, onions, and/or seared pineapple. Alternatively, you can make a semi-sweet dessert by serving the biscuits with diced apples and a little sugar over top.

Ramp and Mushroom Galettes

SERVES 6 TO 8

COOKING IS PERSONAL. I'm the oldest of five children, and being from an itinerant preaching family, we were far from rich. My mother was born in St. Louis and came from a Midwestern Germanic background. Although her mom was a good cook, culinary invention wasn't part of her upbringing, but it became part of ours. My mother learned to make interesting and delicious meals from food that was left on our back porch by parishioners as tithings: bread, rock bass, lard, pork hocks. Mom discovered unusual spices and found a way to make a meal out of everything that was given to us. She learned to cook from the *Woman's Day Encyclopedia of Cookery*, a wonderful set of cookbooks authored by the likes of James Beard, M.F.K. Fisher, and Julia Child. Starting when I was five, my mom and I would open the books and go through them together for hours. I learned to read and cook at the same time. We would talk about Italy and Spain and far-flung parts of the globe, and that was how I learned geography. Cooking has been my world for a very long time.

Every chef has his or her passions, and mine stems from my early years learning the basic tenets of the French culinary canon. Most menus from my formative years included coquilles Saint-Jacques, crêpes suzette, coq au vin, and anything and everything with a demi-glace. Most of those "classics" I now have filed away in the recesses of my repertoire, but one that I still frequently come back to is the Breton galette, a savory buckwheat crêpe. I like to make this recipe in the spring with foraged ramps, but scallions, leeks, or chives can be used in their place quite easily.

1. **MAKE THE MORNAY SAUCE.** Add the milk and mushrooms to a large pot over low heat, and steep for about 5 minutes while you gather the other ingredients and make the roux.

2. In a separate pot, add the butter and cook over medium heat until it begins to brown and has a nutty aroma. Just as it begins to brown, stir in the flour to make a roux. Reduce the heat to medium low, and stir frequently for about 10–15 minutes. The roux should be golden brown when done.

3. Strain the mushrooms from the milk, and whisk the milk into the roux. Discard the mushrooms.

4. Add the onion studded with cloves and cook for 20 more minutes over low heat. Stir in the cheese. Leave on the stove to stay warm.

5. **MAKE THE GALETTES.** Add the eggs to a large bowl and whisk until light and airy. Next, whisk in the flours, then stir in the milk and water a little at a time until the batter just coats the back of a spoon. (The batter should be slightly thicker than classic crêpe batter, but nowhere near as thick as pancake batter.) It should well coat the back of a spoon. You may have to adjust the amount of liquid depending on the moisture content of the flour. Stir in the salt, pepper, and nutmeg.

FOR THE MUSHROOM MORNAY

1¼ cups (313 ml) whole milk

4–5 pieces dried mushrooms

2 tablespoons unsalted butter

2 tablespoons all-purpose flour

Small onion studded with 6 cloves

½ cup (63 g) grated Gruyère or Swiss-style cheese (If you have a local cheese that melts well, and you love the flavor, by all means use that. I often use a local Toussaint cheese from Sprout Creek Farm at the restaurant.)

FOR THE GALETTES

2 large eggs

¾ cup (90g) buckwheat flour

¼ cup (30g) all-purpose flour

2 cups (500 ml) whole milk

1½ cups (375 ml) water

½ teaspoon salt

Pinch of white pepper

Pinch of nutmeg (see Note)

Pat of butter

CONTINUES

6. Add a pat of butter to the bottom of a nonstick pan over medium heat. When the pan is hot and butter melted, ladle in the batter, then twist the pan to coat the bottom of the pan fully, then pour any excess batter from the pan back into the batch through a mesh strainer.

7. Cook until the edges are browned. Flip and cook for 1 minute. Repeat with the remaining batter to make 6 to 8 total galettes.

8. Stack the cooked galettes on a plate and cover with a tea towel. Place in an oven set at 150°F (65°C) to keep warm while you prep the filling.

9. **MAKE THE FILLING.** Julienne the leaves of the ramps and slice the bulbs. Set aside.

10. Add the mushrooms to a dry pan over medium-high heat, and cook until they release their water and start to absorb it back. The mushrooms will be soft and meaty this way.

11. Add the prepared ramps to the mushrooms and drop in the butter. Sauté the mixture for 3 minutes, then add the thyme sprigs, splash of white wine, salt, white pepper, and granulated garlic to taste. Stir to combine. Cook for 3 minutes longer and remove from the heat and set aside.

12. **ASSEMBLE THE GALETTES.** Place each warm galette on an individual plate to be served. Spoon a small amount of the mushroom mornay sauce into the center of each, and then place a portion of the filling on top of the mornay.

13. In a small pan, heat the olive oil over high heat until it begins to smoke. Turn down the heat to medium then crack in two to three eggs at a time, depending on the size of your pan, so the eggs aren't crowded. The eggs will bubble and pop. Baste the eggs with the hot oil until the whites are set. Remove immediately with a slotted spoon and place an egg in the center of each of the fillings. Fold the edges of the galettes inward, leaving the eggs showing in the center.

14. Enjoy with the rest of the white wine!

FOR THE FILLING

12–15 ramps with leaves (Can be replaced with 12–15 scallions or 1 leek.)

12 oyster mushrooms, torn into strips

12 field mushrooms, sliced (I like to use cremini, as they are available year-round, but trumpets, chanterelles, or chicken of the woods are all fantastic.)

2 tablespoons unsalted butter

3 sprigs fresh thyme

1 glass of dry white wine (mostly for you to drink while cooking, but a splash goes into the filling as you cook)

¼ teaspoon salt

Pinch of white pepper

¼ teaspoon granulated garlic

FOR THE EGG TOPPINGS

6 to 8 large eggs (one to top each galette)

¾ cup (180 ml) olive oil

USE WHAT YOU HAVE Buckwheat flour may sit in your cupboard unused after making the galettes. Use it to make a quick bread, like banana buckwheat or oat and cinnamon buckwheat.

NOTE: You'll notice throughout the recipes in this book that I often include nutmeg with my spicing in creamy or delicate dishes. I use the smallest pinch to lend a warm, round note to the dish's finish, which ties all the flavors and aromas together.

Cardoon Mint Bitters

MAKES
4.5 OUNCES

CARDOONS ARE A close cousin of the artichoke and popular in traditional French and Italian rustic dishes. They're also architecturally dramatic—they can grow up to five feet high, and we appreciate the exotic splendor they add to our kitchen garden. This recipe utilizes the cardoon to make a simple astringent bitter reminiscent of an amaro. We like to use it in everything from marinades for pork and beef to cocktails (when added to Campari, it makes a great riff on a negroni). Cheers!

¼ cup peeled and finely chopped cardoon stalk

4 wild mint leaves

2 tablespoons wild mountain thyme

3 teaspoons raspberry leaf

2 tablespoons lemon peel, chopped

2 tablespoons chamomile

2 cardamom pods, crushed

1 teaspoon crushed star anise or fennel seed

5 ounces Everclear alcohol (best) or vodka (usable)

1. Crush the mint, thyme, and raspberry leaf with the back of a chef's knife.

2. Mix all the ingredients in a glass jar.

3. Cover tightly and leave in the refrigerator for a month.

4. Strain before use.

"Last Night's Chinese" Calas

MAKES
6 TO 8 FRITTERS

CALAS ARE AN old New Orleans Creole classic, similar to a beignet but made with rice. There may be no better example of "use what you have and make it magic" than these sweet breakfast treats. If you have rice left over from Chinese food take-out, this is a great next-day use, and I promise there won't be anything left over for the next day.

Sunflower oil to deep fry

1 cup (200 g) cooked white rice

3 large eggs

1 cup (125 g) self-rising flour

½ cup (125 ml) buttermilk or plain yogurt

2 tablespoons organic cane sugar

Pinch of salt

1 teaspoon nutmeg

Confectioners' sugar for dusting

1. Add the sunflower oil to a large pot. The amount of oil depends on the size of your pot—you'll need enough oil to float the fritters. Heat until the oil reaches 325°F (163°C).

2. Meanwhile, mix the rice, eggs, flour, buttermilk, sugar, salt, and nutmeg together in a medium bowl. The final mix should be able to be spooned into the oil and hold its shape. If the batter is too loose, add some more flour. If it's a little thick and glumpy, add more water or buttermilk to thin.

3. Gently drop quenelles (batter spooned into an egg shape) into the hot oil. Don't crowd them. Move the fritters around in the oil and turn over once the bottoms have browned nicely. Continue to check to ensure that the temperature of the oil remains at 325°F (163°C), and continue cooking the fritters until browned on all sides.

4. Remove the calas to a paper towel–lined dish and dab dry. Place them on a serving platter and dust with confectioners' sugar. Serve warm with chicory coffee.

Trout and Salmon Fritters

A COMBINATION OF circumstances led to the final creation of this dish, which has become one of Foxfire's most popular. Originally, these were classic salt cod fritters. Then one Friday, when I went to make a new batch before the restaurant opened, I found that no one had soaked the cod the night before. That was a problem. I scoured the fridge and found a locally smoked trout, but not enough for service. Then I saw we also had a quarter side of locally smoked salmon left over from a recent wedding (we're lucky here in the Catskills that we have some of the finest fish smokers found anywhere—you can't beat Lenny B's smoked trout and Catsmo smoked salmon). In the fridge right next to where I found the salmon was a small container of cumin-and-coriander-dusted boiled potatoes from that morning's breakfast, so those became the main components of what would soon become one of our most requested dishes.

4 small new potatoes, boiled, tossed in butter when warm, and dusted with cumin, ground coriander, salt, and white pepper

6 ounces smoked rainbow trout meat, bones removed

4 ounces chunked or chopped smoked salmon

1 large egg, whisked

½ teaspoon nutmeg

½ cup (65 g) all-purpose flour

½ cup (50 g) bread crumbs

Canola or peanut oil

¼ cup (63 ml) mayonnaise

1 lemon

2 cloves garlic, crushed

½ tablespoon capers, crushed

½ tablespoon finely diced red onion

Pinch of fine sea salt

1. In a medium mixing bowl, crush the cooled potatoes with your hands until you have chunky bits that are no larger than a dime.

2. Add the fish and mix together with your hands. Then, add the egg and nutmeg and blend together. You can use a spoon from here on out if you want.

3. Add enough flour to bring together into a stiff mixture that can easily be formed. Roll the dough into tight golf-ball-size balls.

4. Add the remaining flour and the bread crumbs to two separate pans. Roll the fritters into the flour and then the crumbs. Squeeze the crumbs into the balls and roll one last time in the crumbs.

5. Add about 3 inches of oil to an 8-inch pot and heat to 325°F (163°C). Place the fritters in the oil and fry, turning often, until brown. Place on paper towels to drain.

6. Make a quick aioli by mixing the mayo, juice of half a lemon, garlic cloves, capers, red onion, and salt to taste. Sear off the other half of the lemon in a small pan.

7. Place the fritters on a platter, dollop a bit of aioli on top of each, and serve with the seared lemon on the side.

CHAPTER TWO

MORNING

NOTING.　PLANNING.　COLLECTING.

WALKING THE GARDENS in the morning with a hot cup of coffee in hand, wrapped in a wool shawl if the breeze is cool, is an almost-daily ritual. We're believers in slow and intentional living, even though our lives move fast and we constantly feel like there aren't enough hours in the day to get everything done that we need to do. The risky decision to take charge of our future and work for ourselves in creating Foxfire would be undermined if we didn't find a way to appreciate not only where we are and what we're doing but also to keep growing and getting better. *Mindfulness* and *intentionality* have become trendy catchphrases recently, but the philosophies are vital. Observing small moments, being present and focused, and consistently grateful and open, not only bring awareness and many simple joys, but for us they spark new ideas, too.

Being present in the moment doesn't mean you can't look to the future and ask, *Now, what's next?* And we've found that to be exactly the way design flows: a constant shifting back and forth from the big picture to the details, from the challenges and possibilities of empty rooms in their bare-bones state to the ever-more minute and specific filling of rooms with the actual pieces that will give them life and personality. Once we've created a story for our space and taken the lay of the land, we begin the planning-and-gathering-of-materials stage, a really exciting part of the design process because choices start to get made. The choices you make define the style and character of the room, and it's satisfying to see the design story get written one brush stroke of paint and one item of furniture at a time. ◦

Playing House

IF YOU'RE RENOVATING a room from scratch, your first consideration should be all the fundamental ways a room will be used day to day, so you can decide where outlets, light switches, thermostats, smoke detectors, and light fixtures will go in terms of height and placement. When you move on to decorating the room, these considerations are the same: you will want to think about the size of the space, as well as your own size, so the scale feels right. A home has to be a place where you can rest, and the key to rest is comfort—you, and the occupants of your home, need to fit your space, and your design decisions should facilitate your moving around in it freely and naturally. We have friends with a gorgeous Great Dane, and so when decorating their living room, they had to consider how the dog (who is the size of a small pony) would navigate the areas between chairs and tables without sending everything flying. You have to live comfortably, and your design should enable you to do the things you like to do without being overly precious or concerned with wear and tear, or what's the point?

To make sure you're accounting for these factors, essentially, you need to pretend you're already inhabiting the space. So this is the time to play house and strut your acting chops. First, you need to envision your layout. Because I'm very literal-minded, Tim tapes out the furniture outlines for me, which I find so helpful, and is an extra step that I recommend. We use painter's tape to mark on the floor where the furniture pieces will be positioned (and even light switches, outlets, and wall sconces), doing our best to make it all accurate to scale. If we know we'll have a queen bed in the room, we tape out the exact size of the queen bed in the exact place we plan to put it. Then we tape the placements and sizes for night tables, a dresser, floor lamp, chair, desk, and so on. Next comes acting out a scene in the space.

Will you feel like a nut? Yes, 100 percent. Will you look like a nut? Very definitely. Will you be glad you did it? Yep, and you'll do it every time from now on when you have to design a space. You start by coming into the room and flicking on the pretend light switch—is it in a convenient place or are you walking blindly into the room, groping a wall to find the light? You lie down where the bed will be, and what's your view of the room? Is it the view you want, or do you need to rethink the bed's position? When you get out of bed, is there enough room between the side of the bed and the wall? You get the idea. Really try to envision how that room will look and feel by putting yourself in the scenario. Will the room function comfortably with the way it's going to be used? And if not, how can you make accommodations? For instance, if there's no room for a floor lamp or chair but reading is a priority, then that will affect the lighting choices you'll make. Maybe a swing-arm sconce or a pendant light on each side of the bed would be a better option. Once you've satisfied yourself that the room plan will work by pre-living in it, then it's time to gather the materials. ○

CATSKILL FIELD NOTE MOUNTAINS

GENERAL MEASUREMENT GUIDELINES

Space between bed and wall..minimum 24"

Space needed for pathways through a room................................26"–36"

Space needed in front of a dresser...minimum 24"

Space needed between sofa and coffee table.............................18"

Space needed between two chairs so a table can fit in between............24–42"
(depending on the size of the room)

Space needed from doorway to closest furniture.........................36"

Space needed behind a dining chair..32–36"

Space needed for swing sconces................no more than 36" out from the bed
(and about 20" above the mattress)

Area Rugs Under Beds...should extend 6–12"

Sourcing Materials

AT THE SAME time that we're planning and shaping the spaces into order, we're also shopping, or (ahem) *sourcing* materials and furnishings. We look everywhere and keep an open mind because you never know what you'll find that will be perfect for some space or other, or where you'll come across it. Gathering cool stuff can take a minute, so we're always on the hunt. (We used to have a bumper sticker that read "I Brake for Junk," just saying.) Many times, it's the items we discover that actually trigger the design idea, and not the other way around.

When we bought Foxfire, the property had an abandoned kidney-shaped swimming pool that had been partially bulldozed in, and behind it, an open wood shed. When we came across a whole set of lovely mullioned windows someone had stored in their garage and had put up for sale on Craigslist (thank you, Materials section), we got the idea to use them to enclose the shed and transform it into what we all now call the glass house. The windows mean we can use it all winter long as well. We added one pair of salvaged doors to the front, and a different set to the back, as well as a different door with pretty amber stained glass to the side that leads to the bonfire area. The doors don't match each other or the windows, but that's part of the charm. ○

CATSKILL **FIELD NOTE** MOUNTAINS

SALVAGING OLD WINDOWS AND DOORS

Vintage windows and doors look amazing, but they can be tricky to install into a new space. Here's what we look for when sourcing these items:

1) Be sure the wood isn't rotted, badly split, or peppered with too many nail holes.

2) Check that any decorative molding isn't damaged or missing.

3) For doors, be sure there is room at the top or the bottom to cut down if the doors are too tall or to add wood if too short, since old doors are often non-standard sizes (both in thickness as well as length). Some salvage dealers sell door jambs with the old doors and that can be a time saver.

4) Old paint may contain lead, so use proper precautions if stripping.

5) Check that doors are "square"—90-degree angles on all corners—as they may have warped over time.

6) For windows, think about whether they will be fixed or need to open and which way they'll open.

Creating a Design Pantry

ROOMS ARE ABOUT layering. Just like the pantry in the kitchen has your go-to stable of products that you rely on and use time and again in a variety of different ways, we've created a design pantry that includes key elements that recur throughout all the spaces we design. These are our design staples, our tried-and-true elements that we consistently depend on in the same way that certain ingredients appear again and again in some of your most-loved recipes. But unlike pantry staples, it's a little trickier to figure out your design "ingredients" since there are no recipes to follow.

If you're like us, you have inspiration boards and magazine pics that you've squirreled away for when it's time to decorate, so you're not necessarily starting from zero. (And if you don't, start collecting!) Study those rooms and try to pick out recurring elements, because that's an easy indicator of what you're drawn to. Are you noticing certain colors or wall treatments over and over? If all the rooms in your inspo pics are white, it's probably not the best move to paint your room a dark brooding color, you know? Does a certain style of decor dominate all your pics, like farmhouse or industrial? Or does every living room have a gigantic leather sofa or a curvy velvet chair? Do you have a lot of painted floors or tile floors? Ask yourself not only what do you like, but why do you like it? Break it down

until you can really put your finger on the vibe you want to feel.

So many times, I've seen Tim test a dish he's cooking by sampling a spoonful and then sprinkling in another spice or ingredient to taste. It was like that for us as we developed our own design pantry. We started by looking at bare rooms and very directly asking ourselves what the rooms were lacking, and then we kept improvising "to taste," through trial and error. By using this method, we came up with some starter essentials—texture, pattern, and light—that are the jumping-off point for our designs and that we build decorative layers out from. Design evolves with time and taste, but by starting with these staples, it makes it simpler down the road to change out textiles and small furnishings while leaving the main elements of the room's design timelessly intact. In the big picture, this dressing-the-room step comes after getting a handle on the full space, i.e., identifying the bones. These key elements are like beautiful undergarments before the room's full outfit is put on.

Of course, everyone's style is different, but hopefully seeing how these staples work for us will save you some legwork when creating your own design pantry, since they're initial features to consider for any decor. As with cooking, some ingredients are required right away and some will be stirred into the mix later. ○

(above) Many of the guest rooms at Foxfire have slat walls because it's a simple and inexpensive treatment that adds rustic charm. It complements the building's vintage bones, and the unobtrusive wood texture and slat spacing add definition to the rooms' creamy white walls.

(left) Another great way to create texture on walls is by doing a limewash treatment. We wanted to give this new drywall a richer and older look than just plain paint could achieve. We bought a special accompanying primer and pre-tinted limewash just the way you would buy paint in cans. The application is easy using a long-haired paint brush (never a roller). Keep in mind that limewash paint dries ten times darker than it goes on, so you don't really get a good sense of how it looks until it dries. Keep applying it in thin layers until the rustic old-world finish is to your taste. Be aware that limewash isn't scrubbable, so you either need to use it only in places where you don't anticipate getting fingerprints or cooking splatters, or top coat with polyurethane or wax to finish.

TEXTURE

Texture is what we give first priority as we've found that switching up or adding texture to a room can be the biggest game changer. As soon as we started to consider textural options for the bones of the room—the walls, floor, and ceiling—the rooms immediately gained more personality and presence. Once we looked beyond the basic smooth drywall option for walls and ceiling, things got exciting. It might be just one key wall that gets a texture treatment, or it might be all four, but we now plaster, panel, tile, wallpaper, stencil, or a combination of those in every room we design to add immediate style. Adding wood strips and/or beams to ceilings, molding, or wallpaper all make for rewarding transformations. I should mention the caveat that at times, smooth drywall may be the right choice, like in an ultra-modern space, but then I'd be sure to include lots of textured furnishings, wall hangings, and art, as well as sculptural lighting.

PATTERN

Pattern and texture go hand in hand. Like texture, pattern can be used to create interesting features, and while it can come later, in the form of fabrics for pillows and furnishings, it can also be used in this first layer of the room's design. When laying a wood floor, for example, consider options other than just the classic strip-flooring design. The sky's the limit: herringbone, concentric boxes, basket weave, inlay, or different color wood stains are all great options. The only thing to keep in mind is that the showier the pattern is, the simpler the other elements in the room should be so they're not all competing for attention. You're aiming for balance.

(below) I love wallpaper, but I'm still a little afraid of it. I worry that I'll get bored with the pattern and it's kind of a hassle to hang, especially as a do-it-yourselfer who doesn't do it often enough to get really good at it. That said, I've always loved the results, and many great wallpapers now just peel off if you want to make a change. I tend to fall for expensive handmade papers that need cutting and glue though, so you have to be in the mood to take on the project, measuring accurately and being precise. We hung a bold navy-and-white wallpaper on a feature wall in one of our guest rooms that's called "Fox in the Snow" and is made by Lake August. Our guests regularly request the "fox room" and pose for pictures in front of the wallpaper. We could only afford to do one wall, but it makes a big impact and we've not remotely tired of it yet.

(**opposite**) We like to think of the ceiling as a fifth wall, and adding texture to the ceiling with beadboard, tin, or paneling can also work wonders. In the lounge, we added beadboard panels and beams for decoration rather than support. Black ceilings can make many rooms feel claustrophobic, but it works in this living area to create a cozy and intimate place to hang out for the guests, especially partnered with the gray walls and a black floor. It's the only dark space we have at Foxfire, and it makes a nice contrast to the light and bright guest rooms and other common spaces.

(**above**) The same goes for the floor—it can be treated as another wall when looking to add texture to the box of the room. We love wood plank flooring, and we're obsessed with tiles: tiles in general, anywhere and everywhere! We've used a ton of tiling at Foxfire and it's become a memorable aspect of the overall design.

Creating Tile "Carpets"

AS YOU KNOW by now, reusing and repurposing is part of everything we do. It makes sense for the planet and it makes sense for our budget. We frequent flea markets, yard sales, antiques stores, and we love all the online sources for vintage finds. Although these places are great for scoring unique furnishings and accessories for finishing touches, you can also find raw materials that are perfect for adding texture and pattern to a room in the initial stages of design.

One day, Tim was poking around in the Materials section of Craigslist when he found a huge mixed lot of tiles for sale—patterned cement, unglazed clay, glazed clay—in a bunch of assorted shapes and sizes. A truckload of tiles for $3,500. Most were 8 x 8-inch squares, but there were subway tiles and hexagons and little squares, too. The seller couldn't say for certain how many tiles there were in total, or how many different patterns, or the quantity of each pattern, and we didn't have $3,500 to spare for a zillion tiles that we didn't have any actual need or plan for.

We hemmed and hawed for a week, going back and looking at the seller's blurry pictures, debating the merits and brainstorming ideas. They did look kind of amazing, and we still had all the bathroom floors, commercial kitchen, and the back-entrance foyer flooring to solve. We decided to take the plunge and do what we usually do, which is to buy what we love and figure out later what to do with it. Today, it's fair to say we can't imagine how Foxfire would look without these tiles.

They played an important part in the first, and most special, DIY project we ever did at Foxfire, which was to tile the 72-foot-long front veranda. When we bought the place, the old wood veranda was rotted and collapsing, so first we made it structurally sound. The truckful of tiles arrived right when we were figuring out what sort of flooring to lay. Because we didn't know how many of each pattern we had, it meant sorting the heavy cement tiles into like piles, which was backbreaking work. It soon became very clear that we didn't have enough of any one pattern or color to tile the whole veranda.

We came up with the idea of "carpets" of tile out of necessity. We lugged the tiles this way and that way, changing the patterns until we settled on a design that looked nice, but most important, would work given our limitations in terms of tile numbers. Tim came up with the idea of using plain tiles as a border and as dividers between the different patterned "carpets" when we ran short on the patterned tiles. After all the tiles were laid in place, Tim then took on properly setting them. With no tiling experience whatsoever, it took him three weeks to lay all the tile. Tim notes now that he should

have started at the far end of the long veranda and worked his way back instead of starting at the front part that everyone sees when they arrive, since by the time he got to the end he was pretty good and the tiles were set more evenly. Live and learn. (Or watch more YouTube videos before starting.) ○

TILING TIPS

1. Have 15 percent extra tiles on hand for damage and mistakes.

2. Where possible, use tile mastic instead of thin-set mortar until you get more experienced, as it's more forgiving and won't leave you with lips between the tiles.

3. Two indispensable tools are a wet saw for smoothly cutting the tiles and a good grinder with a tile blade for making small corner and intricate cuts.

4. Use good quality screw-down tile spacers and levelers to give you a perfectly level floor.

5. Start tiling in the least obvious place so you can get your technique down.

6. If doing patterns using different tiles, the key is to make sure the tile thickness is the same or it's a lot trickier to get it all level.

We picked up the lot of tiles from a warehouse in Brooklyn in three trips. We used these tiles as stair risers, bathroom and kitchen flooring, the kitchen walls, fireplace wall, and with what was leftover, we made a beautiful patchwork dancefloor for the weddings we host. It's safe to say that the tiles allowed us to create a special, patterned element that set these rooms apart (and that sometimes, buy now, think later, is a perfectly acceptable design plan).

LIGHT

After we've used texture and pattern to give character to the bones of the room, the next key element is to bring in light by incorporating unique built-in ceiling fixtures and hard-wired wall lights. Successful rooms contain more than one source of lighting and different shades of light, from bright to dim. Lighting is the room's jewelry, and a great way to make a style statement that sets the tone and is a shorthand for the overall design vibe you want the room to have. Contrasts can be so effective here, either in style, like using a modern chandelier in an old-world room or hanging a crystal chandelier in a barn, or with size, by using an under- or oversize light fixture where you wouldn't normally expect it. It's a fast track to high style.

Because light fixtures can be expensive, we're always creating our own. We're the ones you'll see in a store turning wicker baskets, vases, or plant pots upside down and holding them up in the air to see what they'd look like as pendant lights. Just add a cord kit and you're done. Whatever you can dream up, there's a way to make it. We find light fixtures can add a touch of worldly glamour to a space, too, whether that be a Moroccan lantern or a Japanese rice paper shade or a gothic Spanish chandelier. The right light fixture is a punctuation mark in the narrative of the room, and as much as they can set the tone for the overall design theme, they can also be their own thing, functioning as an interesting aside to the room's conversation.

One thing we actually give thought to is the choice of lightbulb, since the color quality will change the look of all the furnishings, not to mention the people, in the space. We generally go for warm white or amber bulbs for softness in the guest rooms. Silver-bottom bulbs and crystal-look bulbs are perfect choices for pendants where the bulbs are very noticeable. And dimmers are the absolute best for every room, so you can control the mood.

While on the subject of lighting, consider the switch plates in each room, and whether you want

(below) We bought some bone-inlay switch plates on sale at Anthropologie that add a nice touch of the exotic to the wall. Wrought-iron, steel, and copper switch plates can all look good as well.

(opposite) Another way to keep costs down is to buy ceiling fixtures and lamps vintage. Just make sure the wiring is not ancient and scary looking. We bought this shell pendant light at an antiques store in New Jersey, and even though the Catskills are far from the beach, the vibe still fits the overall aesthetic that nature rules and is worth showcasing.

(following) We like to give the outside properties a warm glow with a combination of string lights, gas lanterns, and dark-sky approved porch lights.

them to be noticed or disappear into the background. There are some really nice alternatives out there to the builder's usual. If you'd rather have them blend in, we're all for painting out the switch plates and outlet covers to the same color as the wall to make them barely noticeable. ○

RECIPES

JUST AS WE have our staples in the design pantry, Tim has some staples in his kitchen pantry that he uses time and again in the meals we serve. Tim is always playing around with creating new spice blends, as well as preserving essential ingredients, both of which he stores and uses in upcoming dishes. This further illustrates our philosophy of use what you have (and make magic with it!) and also helps us feel confident about where some of the ingredients come from, since we grew them ourselves and know how they were processed.

Foxfire Harissa Spice Powder

MAKES 1 CUP

EVERY CHEF HAS his or her own secret blend of seasoning that gives their food a signature taste. Sometimes this isn't a conscious thing but rather just the flavors they like that get repeated in many of the dishes they cook. Over the centuries, some of these blends have become classics like garam masala, Chinese five-spice, herbes de Provence, Old Bay seasoning, and filé Creole seasoning.

At Foxfire, I have a caddy of spices that I prepare at the beginning of each day. The range of spices, to me, is like the paint on an artist's palette. My spice caddy contains freshly ground nutmeg, coarse sea salt, fine sea salt, granulated garlic, Korean chili flakes, cinnamon, smoked paprika, butcher-grind black pepper, fine-ground black pepper, white pepper, cumin, and coriander. The caddy sits by the stove, and I pinch up whatever feels right for the dish, adding and stirring as I go. Each day, I may add additional spices to the caddy depending upon that day's menu, but these are my staples.

I also like to make compound spice blends that I store in the pantry for future use. This is a derivation of a harissa powder that I like to keep on hand for use in eggplant dishes, especially our Eggplant with Harissa on page 158.

2 tablespoons cumin seeds

2 tablespoons coriander seeds

1 teaspoon caraway seeds

½ cup (312 g) Korean red pepper flakes

2 tablespoons smoked paprika

1 tablespoon ground cinnamon

1 tablespoon fine sea salt

1 tablespoon coarse sea salt

1 tablespoon garlic

½ teaspoon ground cloves

1 teaspoon ground white pepper

1. Toast the cumin, coriander, and caraway seeds in a dry pan over medium-low heat until fragrant.

2. Remove the seeds from the heat and, using a mortar and pestle or spice grinder, grind them into a powder.

3. Transfer the powdered seeds into a bowl, then add the remaining ingredients. Mix thoroughly to combine.

4. Store in an airtight container for future use. It will keep for about six months.

Canned Tomatoes with Basil and Fennel Fronds

MAKES
4 QUARTS

KITCHEN GARDENS ARE wonderful things, full of color, flavor, and all possibilities of future culinary greatness. They're also finicky, time-consuming, and demanding, so when a carefree, highly productive, and delicious plant comes along, I can't help but celebrate it. Such are the small, viny tomatoes of the cherry, grape, and pear varieties. They grow easily and are so prolific that it can be hard to keep up with the quantity produced. This is why we like to preserve the explosive flavors of our homegrown tomatoes to be enjoyed down the road.

These canned tomatoes work great in quick salsas, sauté pasta sauces, bruschetta, and any stew dish that needs some extra acidic zest.

4 sprigs fresh basil

8 to 12 cups (1 to 2 pounds) small heirloom tomatoes, including grape and cherry

4 cloves garlic, peeled

1 medium onion, chopped

4 medium fennel fronds

4 bay leaves

1 tablespoon fennel seed

2 tablespoons pickling salt

1 cup (250 ml) apple cider vinegar

1 tablespoon cane sugar

4 cups (1 L) water

1. Wash and snip basil leaves from their stems. Discard stems and set leaves aside.

2. Wash the tomatoes under cold running water and remove any stems or leaves. Using a thin metal skewer, prick the stem end of each tomato.

3. Wash four quart-size canning jars in hot water. Into each of the four jars, put a quarter of the basil, a clove of peeled garlic, a quarter of the onion, 1 fennel frond, 1 bay leaf, 1 teaspoon fennel seed, and ½ tablespoon pickling salt.

4. Pack the tomatoes into the jars, leaving a half inch of headspace at the top of each jar.

5. Combine the vinegar, sugar, and water in a medium pot. Bring to a boil and remove from the heat.

6. Fill the jars with the hot vinegar mixture, making sure to retain the half inch of headspace. Wipe the jar rims and seal with lids. These will keep for about a year, until the next season.

Lebanese-Style Preserved Lemon

**MAKES
1 QUART**

PRESERVED LEMONS HAVE a flavor that is at once earthy, exotic, and bright. Salt combines with the lemon juice to act as a pickling agent, which softens the rind's texture and rounds out its flavor. I like to use preserved lemons to balance the richness of lamb or enliven simple bean dishes. Consider combining them with raisins, almonds, spinach, or beets to create delicious sides and garnishes.

4–5 medium lemons

½ cup (130 g) fine sea salt

1 tablespoon Himalayan pink salt

1 whole clove

1 teaspoon coriander seeds

1 teaspoon black peppercorns

1 bay leaf

1 cup (250 ml) fresh-squeezed lemon juice, if needed

1. Slice each lemon into quarters by cutting from the top tip down to a half inch from the bottom so that the four slices are connected at the base.

2. Gently spread open the lemon slices and rub the sea salt on the exposed flesh, then close the lemon back up.

3. Place the Himalayan pink salt at the bottom of a quart-size mason jar. Pack in the lemons one at a time, sprinkling in more sea salt as well as the clove, coriander, and peppercorns between layers. Tuck in the bay leaf. Press the lemons down to release their juices and to make room for the remaining lemons. If the juice released from the squashed fruit does not cover them completely, add freshly squeezed lemon juice as needed, leaving a half inch of headspace. Seal the jar.

4. Let the lemons preserve for a month in a warm place, shaking daily to distribute the salt and juice. Before use, rinse the lemons under cold running water and pat them dry. These will keep for about a year, until the next season.

Charred Pickled Fennel

MAKES
3 PINTS

WE HEART FENNEL, underappreciated as it is. Great pickled cucumbers or beets are easy to come by in the Hudson Valley, but preserved fennel not so much. We regularly make our own that's crave-worthy: slightly crisp and briny with a hint of sweet anise and a caramelized char. We use hits of pickled fennel to enhance pasta sauces, stews, fish dishes, and we like to add it to a simple repast of wine and cheese just the way you would any pickle out of the jar.

1. Slice the fennel bulb into thirds.

2. Heat the olive oil in a cast-iron pan over medium-high heat. Add the fennel and char on all sides. Set aside.

3. In a separate pot, combine the vinegar, sugar, water, and sea salt and bring to a boil over high heat.

4. Lower the heat to medium and add the fennel. Cook the fennel for about 3–4 minutes, until it is partially cooked and just soft on the outside.

5. Place a third of the celery seeds, caraway seeds, red pepper flakes, and mustard seeds in the bottom of three pint-size mason jars. Remove the fennel from the pot with tongs, and pack a third of it into each jar along with a sprig of thyme. Fill each jar with the hot vinegar solution, leaving a half inch of headspace.

6. Let the fennel marinate for at least a week before using. It will keep for about a year, until the next season.

¾ pound of fennel (1 medium-size bulb)

⅜ cup (94 ml) extra-virgin olive oil

2 cups (500 ml) white distilled or wine vinegar (5% acidity)

⅔ cup (135 g) granulated sugar

⅓ cup (84 ml) water

1 teaspoon coarse sea salt

1 teaspoon each of whole celery seeds, whole caraway seeds, red pepper flakes, and yellow mustard seeds

3 sprigs fresh thyme

Oil-Cured Canned Mackerel

MAKES
2 PINTS

TO ME, MACKEREL is sustainable, inexpensive, abundant, healthy, and delicious. It sometimes gets a bad rap for being too strong or "fishy," but the truth is that there is a wide range in flavor depending on the type and size. For this dish, I like to use a younger and smaller Atlantic mackerel, but any variety will do (as will other fish like salmon, bluefish, or albacore).

A quick aside on sustainability of our fish population. We sometimes struggle to determine what fish is best; can I eat swordfish now or later? How about yellowfin tuna? A simple rule of thumb that I use is the smaller the fish, the safer it is. Less mercury means better rebounding of the population. Being a Northeasterner and a onetime fishmonger, I regularly cook with bluefish, mackerel, sardine, smelt, albacore, trout, arctic char, and hake.

1. Heat a dry cast-iron pan over medium-high heat. Add two sliced rings of the onion, and brown on both sides. Set aside.

2. Heat the olive oil in a large pot over medium heat. Add the garlic and half the fennel (or basil leaves), and gently sauté for a minute to combine. Add the crushed tomatoes and red pepper flakes. Simmer for 15 minutes, stirring occasionally. Set aside.

3. Place one grilled onion ring in the bottom of two pint-size mason jars.

4. Cut the mackerel into 3½-inch lengths and split the fish between the jars.

5. Place a fennel frond (or basil leaf) in each jar and add half the salt, black peppercorns, and caraway seeds to each jar.

6. Add the warm tomato sauce to each jar, leaving a one inch of headspace.

7. Carefully clean the jar rims and remove any fish oil from the outside of the jars. Seal with the lids.

8. Process in a pressure canner at eleven pounds pressure for 1 hour and 40 minutes. It will keep about a year.

¼ medium onion, cut into rings

1 tablespoon olive oil

2 garlic cloves, crushed

4 fennel fronds (or 4 basil leaves)

12 ounces crushed tomatoes

1 teaspoon red pepper flakes

1 pound mackerel filets, skinned and deboned

1 teaspoon fine sea salt

1 teaspoon cracked black peppercorns

1 teaspoon caraway seeds

NOTE: Fish, even in tomato, needs to be pressure canned. This is not as scary as it sounds. A pressure canner is different from a pressure cooker, but modern dual-use electric canner/cookers are available at a reasonable price, and having one adds a lot of variety to your canning options.

USE WHAT YOU HAVE Use this canned mackerel preserve to make a tasty pasta dish by warming it in a pan along with some of your preserved tomatoes (page 101), throwing in some peas, and adding a healthy dose of olive oil. It's also a tasty snack chopped into a salad to top crisp rye crackers and paired with a glass of Kabinett-style Riesling. But my favorite way to eat this is to pulse it in a food processor and then spread it on a toasted baguette topped with shaved pecorino Romano cheese.

Quick Simple Kimchi

MAKES
2 QUARTS

THERE IS A wonderful satisfaction that comes from eating fermented foods: consider bread, beer, wine, salami, pickles, sauerkraut, and arguably the king of all fermented things, kimchi. Sour and spicy with a soft texture, kimchi is incredibly versatile. I like to use it to flavor rice bowls, tacos, scrambled eggs, and even sandwiches like grilled cheese.

The recipe below uses a full head of napa cabbage, but you can alter this to a half or quarter head if that's what you happen to have left over from another dish. Kimchi is a great way to preserve cabbage (or other vegetables) for an extended period since it will last a month in the fridge after fermentation. As it ages, the flavor intensity only deepens.

1. Core and cut the cabbage into quarters lengthwise, then cut crosswise into two-inch squares.

2. In a large bowl, toss the cabbage with the salt until the cabbage just starts to wilt. Pour in enough cold water to cover. Mix periodically for about 2 hours.

3. Rinse the cabbage well, then drain. Squeeze any remaining water from the cabbage and return it to the bowl.

4. In a food processor or blender, puree the garlic, ginger, and sugar with the fish sauce until smooth.

5. Pour the mixture over the cabbage. Add the red pepper flakes, gochujang, and scallions and toss to coat. Add the radish or pear to the cabbage mixture and toss again. Marinate at least 1 hour.

6. Split the kimchi between two quart-size mason jars with the lids on loosely so they don't pop as they ferment. Set the jars on a sheet pan to catch any juice as it bubbles up and flows over. Allow to sit at room temperature for 2 days. Taste every few days until it's perfect to you. For a softer and tarter kimchi, let stand for up to 5 days. Each day, remove the lids to release gases and press down to keep the mixture submerged. Refrigerate until ready to use.

1 medium head napa cabbage

¼ cup (130 g) kosher or fine sea salt

5–6 garlic cloves

2 tablespoons peeled fresh ginger

1 teaspoon granulated sugar

2 tablespoons fish sauce or salted shrimp paste

3 tablespoons gochujang

2 teaspoons Korean red pepper paste

4 medium scallions, trimmed and cut into one-inch pieces

8 ounces daikon radish or Asian pear, peeled and cut into matchsticks

CHAPTER THREE

DAY

CREATION.   TRANSFORMATION.   EVOLUTION.

BEFORE WE MET, Tim lived in a house that was off the grid, and it's taken on the allure of legend now in our household. My husband is rugged and handsome, and I have this pioneering mountain-man image of him as he speaks fondly of waking in the night to stoke the wood fire to keep the house warm, or reading novels by kerosene lamps in the evenings. Tim had to be consciously mindful of light, water, and heat, and they all took consistent effort. He had to work to live, literally, and for him that was a labor of love.

Until Foxfire, "labor of love" wasn't a phrase I ever used personally or even thought much about. It implies you love what you're doing on a soul level, enough so that you don't need to be paid for it. The reward is in the work itself, despite it being hard. Foxfire would be a million tasks with no recompense in sight except for the hopeful promise of travelers on down the road coming to stay overnight, to drink and dine, listen to records, hang out by the fire. I imagined globe-trotters and wanderers, creatives and bankers, young and old coming to stay in this place we were making day by day. Everything we did was with these imagined guests in mind. I didn't love the labor, but I did labor out of love.

From the beginning, Foxfire was never about making money to get rich, it was about making a living so that Tim and I could be together more and not need to hold outside jobs. The renovation work was hard and dirty and slow—everything took longer than we thought it would. Most things cost more than we thought they would. But we had big hopes for the future. Of course, we talked about worst-case scenarios all the time. What if we ran out of money and the renovation never got finished? What if we built it and no one came? What if people came but then didn't enjoy themselves? I'm the worst sort of risk-taker because I worry the whole time yet can't help myself from diving into staggering challenges. Tim likes to quote (and live by) Ray Bradbury's line, "Jump off the cliff and build your wings on the way down." If you quit mid-plummet, without your wings fully formed, you end in a splattered mess, so we kept moving forward step by step, decision by decision.

There is no romance to the restrictions we faced of money, time, or even our own handyman skills, but those obstacles have proven to be the most reliable triggers to our creativity. We always start with: Can a thing be saved or reused? Can it be reinvented or repurposed? Can we do it ourselves? We think outside the box because we've had to for so long to make our goals happen, to keep our creations original, and, ideally, to make them lastingly beautiful, as well. The next phase of the design process is where the spaces get dressed, the basic clothing over the undergarments. With the major architectural renos completed, this is when the cosmetic transformations happen—choosing colors, furniture, and top-level accessories. It's when the rooms really start to take shape. ○

Paint Alchemy

WHEN ALL ELSE fails, there's nothing like the power of paint to transform a room or an object. It's not an exaggeration to say that I've had paint in my hair to some extent for at least the past two years. I'm always painting or tinkering with things, adding or taking away from them, changing them into a better version of themselves. To me, painting an object is a kind of design alchemy, a magic that happens when something really amazing blooms from something that wasn't so good in its raw state.

In addition to personal preference, there are other factors to consider when choosing paint colors: the kind of natural light the room gets, the room's use, and the color tones of the furnishings all come into play. Over the years, we've painted everything from brick house exteriors to wall tiles to a bathroom countertop to a canoe. Paint is without a doubt the ultimate way to make a change without spending a fortune.

While starting with the paint color seems like a good plan, we actually prefer to start by choosing a key item that will be featured in the room and then choosing the color as a complement to that. For one thing, it narrows down the paint color options, making life a lot easier, and second, it keeps you from going through the trouble of painting the whole room and then bringing in the intended sofa, curtains, or artwork to find the walls aren't exactly the shade you intended. It's way better to color coordinate the paint to the item first. If you have no plan at all yet for what will be in the room, then create a palette so that you can choose the paint color and the furniture pairings with confidence. The palette can come from wardrobe items you like to wear together or a painting you love that you can pull colors out of to use as your guide for picking pieces of furniture and paint.

We don't abide by the purists who think wood paneling should never be violated with paint. Not that we don't get a little pang with the first brushstroke or two (we're human). True, sometimes wood is beautiful as wood. But sometimes it's better painted.

When we acquired Foxfire, the main floor had two principal large areas: the lounge and the dining room. Between them was an entrance foyer that would become the lobby. The floors didn't match or flow between the rooms. All the floors were hardwood, but the strips of wood in the living room had been painted beige; the floors in the lobby were the original Douglas fir with faded outlines of red, green, and gold harlequin color blocks; and the dining room was left natural. We estimated the flooring throughout to be about 120 years old, and the structure was very basic and lacking a subfloor. This meant that the floor wasn't thick enough to withstand sanding to remove the paint in the lounge, so we had to make do with paint to tie the look together and make the lounge floor feel cozy enough for our guests to want to cocoon in front of the roaring fire night after night. ○

CATSKILL   **FIELD NOTE**   MOUNTAINS

FOXFIRE'S GO-TO BASIC PAINT COLORS

Picking paint colors is one of life's challenges destined to either break you or make you stronger. Through all the work we've done, we now have some favorite go-to colors that we intend to use forever and ever, or at least until they're discontinued.

WHITES: Benjamin Moore "Simply White" and Sherwin Williams "Dover White"

GRAYS: Benjamin Moore "Bone Black" and Sherwin Williams "Mink"

BLACKS: Sherwin Williams "Sealskin" and "Black Magic"

DIY | "De-stressed" Painted Wood Floors | WHAT WE LEARNED ALONG THE WAY

IN GENERAL, I love painted floors. I think they look cottagey and have an honest, welcoming simplicity. At first, we decided to paint the lounge and lobby floors to match and leave the dining room's natural brown hardwood. We looked at so many shades of gray and white, but somehow we ended up deciding to paint the floors a striking rich, glossy black. We put beadboard panels on the ceiling and painted those the same shade of black to tie the room together.

We painted ourselves backward out of the rooms and finally ended up at the door to the veranda, where we gazed with admiration at what we'd done. It really was a beautiful look . . . until the next morning.

It was impossible. Literally everything showed on the floor. You couldn't take a step without a white footprint appearing. Dirt showed, dust showed. It was a disaster, a beautiful disaster. But Tim believes everything is fixable. He came up with

the idea to distress the floors so imperfections would be harder to spot. He got down on his knees with a hand sander and went over the paint to lightly wear down the areas where the wood would have naturally weathered because it was raised a little higher or was in a natural traffic area. Hand sanding dulled the gloss and let some wood show through and, most importantly, meant you could now walk across the floor without leaving dramatic footprints with every step. We joked that the method should be called *de-stressing* instead of distressing since that's what it accomplished. ○

DISTRESSING TIPS

1. Lightly sand the floors with 150-grit sandpaper, wash them down to get rid of the sawdust, and apply a layer of primer.

2. Use a specialty porch or floor paint and apply a thin first coat. When dry, apply a second thin coat.

3. Let dry for three days—the paint must be super dry and hard so it can withstand the sanding without peeling.

4. Use a light touch with a hand sander to go over the boards, passing back and forth where there are raised edges or in natural traffic areas for a warm, worn look.

(opposite) One thing that happened at first by accident, and then later deliberately, is that we like to include a touch of black in every space. It doesn't even have to be a lot, like the back plate of these massive antlers in Foxfire Cottage, but especially in lighter spaces, the black grounds the whole room and toughens it up in a crisp, sharp way.

(above) In contrast to the lounge, we decided to paint the wood floors in the guest rooms a creamy white color that brightened the rooms substantially. It may seem as though choosing white as a paint color is a way to opt out of making a harder color decision, but for us, white was as much a color choice as any other. It was a gamble to paint floors white, especially when we knew they'd get a lot of foot traffic, but the maintenance is worth it. Foxfire is more than a hundred years old and made of wood. You will inevitably hear floorboards creak and sounds through walls. But it's perfectly imperfect in its way. The white rooms have a calm airiness to them that creates a positive, happy feel, especially when the sun is shining and they appear to glow with light.

We love the drama of black window frames and have used them effectively in various rooms. They're as timeless as white window frames and add a crisp modern contrast to lighter walls, plus the frames disappear to showcase the outside views.

CATSKILL FIELD NOTE MOUNTAINS

PAINT SAMPLES

When choosing a paint color, we're usually deciding between shades of one color and not a bunch of very different colors. We learned the hard way that painting a few test patches on a wall quickly led to us forgetting which was which. Now, before we start, we label the paint cans with numbers that correspond to the numbers on our test swatches.

Found and Foraged

THE BEAUTY AND benefits of reusing, repurposing, and reinventing aren't new, but I'll add our voice to say we've found it to be the best way to incorporate high-quality and unique items on a budget.

If we picked furniture and lighting only from big brand-name stores, a mood board (a curated selection of images that evoke the vibe we're trying to create for each room) would be useful and easy to make. But when we decorate a room, we don't create a specific mood board since we don't know exactly what we're going to find when we go antiquing and flea market shopping. Rather, we go armed with a basic understanding of how the room will be used, who will use it, and the story of the space (page 18). Then we go out shopping and see what we can find.

The velvet sofa we might score at a low price and in perfect condition means we're living with its mustard color, since everything comes as is and is one of a kind. That sofa in that mustard color and style then affects the color of paint we use and the type of lamps we buy, and that affects the colors in the rug, and so on as the design choices naturally get narrower and simpler as you purchase your key pieces for a room. We decided early on that vintage was economical, and since the furniture would get hard commercial use, it could be replaced or given updates as needed to stay fresh and current.

Heirloom and modern pieces both have a place in our designs. We're always looking for elements that will round out a room and create a timeless and unified look. Filling a room with flea market finds can quickly border on shabby and hodge-podge; instead, we prefer a mix of old and new to keep the spaces unique and comfortable. We're not snobby at all about where to shop, and we like the hunt for stylish items at home-goods retail stores as much as we do at antiques stores. There are only a couple of things I can think of that we'll always buy new: mattresses and toilet seats. We furnished Foxfire with at least 80 percent vintage items. They age well and let guests relax comfortably. Nicks and scratches, even the odd nearly threadbare armrest, allow people to feel at home and not worry too much about putting their feet up on the coffee table. The lounge has vintage velvet sofas that still look great two years down the road. We had a thing for a while with yellow velvet, and we have a sofa in the lounge and a love seat in one of the guest rooms that went along with that theme. The navy velvet sofa by the fireplace is a coveted hangout spot for relaxing. The old sofas are soft and slouchy, and when we get tired of them, it won't break the bank to replace them.

Although we're always on the hunt for pieces with good bones, I will say we're careful not to take on too many "project" purchases. It's the quickest route to a locker full of unused stuff—chairs that need recovering; lamps that need rewiring; table-tops that need legs—all bought with a good creative plan that is somehow never realized. Now we will only buy a project piece if we know for certain we can tackle it immediately.

Sometimes it feels like our lives revolve around

stuff: getting rid of it and getting more of it. With all the guest rooms and main spaces we had to fill, we've had to purchase a lot of furniture, and so going to outdoor flea markets and antiques shows, where there's a huge selection of stuff in one place and at pretty good prices, is what dreams are made of. Dealers have packed up all their wares in their vehicles and lugged it all to the show, and you know they don't want to lug it all back with them. So there are deals to be had for sure, and you can't be shy about negotiating.

You're not insulting the dealer by asking what their best price is. They expect you to ask. I have my own personal trick for getting something I really want as cheaply as possible: I make Tim go ask. It's not that I'm too shy or nervous to negotiate—I've worked on enough antiques-picking shows in television to feel comfortable with that whole process, which is really just a game—it's that I have an obvious tell. One look at me, one look into my smitten and fevered eyes, and the dealer knows without a doubt that I've shopped all morning and this is the exact item I want to buy because I love it. I would probably pay more than the asking price for it. So I have Tim go talk to the seller while I amble away pretending to look at other things, still within earshot. Tim can feign a confident nonchalance like he could take or leave the item and it wouldn't matter a bit, and he uses this phrasing: "I need your very best price on this." Somehow he always gets it. I think it's the word *need* that works for him. Not the usual query of "What's your best price for this?" But "I *need* your *very best* price on this." Try it, and you're welcome.

I could write chapters and chapters on how to tell good-quality pieces from junk. But there are a million books out there on the topic, and in the end, unless you're reselling it or keeping the item for the

Beautiful details can take time to find in antiques stores and flea markets, since we're always looking for pieces that are "right" and will fit into the overall design.

rest of your life, does it matter if it only holds up for a couple more years of use? If you love it, buy it and enjoy it with no regrets. That said, it feels really good to buy a piece that's "right," as one of the hosts of a picking show I worked on used to say. We'd be climbing through an old barn or attic, and he'd pick up an item and say, "This is *right*," or sometimes "This is *good*." It usually meant the piece was an authentic antique, not a reproduction, something relatively rare and collectible and worth buying on the show so viewers could learn about its history. I have that too when I'm shopping, a feeling that this is *right*. But while I was still honing that sense, I relied on a few tried-and-true tips. ○

CATSKILL · FIELD NOTE · MOUNTAINS

FLEA MARKET TIPS

- Arrive early in the morning for the best selection and head to the spot farthest away from the entrance first, since almost everyone will start browsing at the front. There will be more selection, though not necessarily the best bargains yet. That comes later in the afternoon, when dealers want less to pack up and will slash prices to make that happen.

- Try to buy more than one item from any dealer. The more items you bundle together, the better the overall price you're likely to get.

- Don't think you'll get a better price by dissing the thing you want to buy. If the price isn't low enough, you can point out chips or flaws, but do it nicely, like "I wish the hinge wasn't broken so the door would close properly." A little passive-aggressive behavior can work in these situations, but if you complain too much about it, the dealer will just think you shouldn't buy it.

- Ask questions about the item you like: Where did it come from? How old is it? Show interest to engage the seller so they're more inclined to want to have the piece go home with you. They bought it in the first place because they thought it was "right" and will be pleased that you think so too.

- Finally, keep a little package of wet wipes with you, since stuff is often dirty and your hands will get grimy from touching everything.

QUICK WAYS WE USE TO KNOW IF A PIECE IS "RIGHT"

- **WEIGHT**: Old pieces often weigh more than newer reproductions.

- **CRAFTSMANSHIP**: Beautiful joinery (dovetail joints) and finishing details (molding that has worn and softened with age; nails that have lost their shine).

- **PATINA**: Is the item dirty enough and worn in the right areas? Old things get dirty in a kind of beautiful way as the wood darkens or the luster of gilding mellows. Old items were less factory-made than new, so imperfections happened by the maker's hand.

- **STURDINESS**: Are the legs loose and wobbly? Turn the piece over to see if screws can be tightened easily to fix. Everything can be fixed, but do you want to bother? We often walk away from wobbly, as that signifies a more structural, rather than cosmetic, fix.

If You Can't Find It, Make It

IN OUR WORLD, custom-made usually means beautiful but too pricey for our budget, so we've had to create our own designs when we wanted a unique piece. From the outset, we knew that beds were going to be all-important, since we'd have fourteen rooms, and let's face it, the bed is the key feature of any hotel room. The goal was to make the beds as attractive as they were sturdy. I wanted them to look rustic and natural, a modern platform style with a vintage vibe. I loved the idea of a pioneer rope bed and was quite fixed on that, but then all the research I did warned that the ropes inevitably stretch out, causing the bed to bow and the mattress to sag.

Everything requires constant compromise and improvisation, so we sketched up a very simple platform frame with tapered legs and hemp rope details, which gave the illusion of the rope bed but with the more modern structural support of wood slats. We showed our pencil sketches to an aging local carpenter, an ex–Greenwich Village beatnik, who drove up on his motorcycle and smoked a lot of cigarettes while he flipped through our drawings. We said we wanted the bed frame to be rustic and rugged and simple. Barn board would be perfect. After a long draw on his cigarette, he said he'd be able to source naturally sun-bleached boards from his friend's falling-down bull pen.

We immediately fell in love with the beautiful gray wood boards when he pulled up later that week with them piled into the open back of his pal's rusty pickup truck. For almost a month,

he worked every day building the beds using a couple of sawhorses, tools, and tarps that he'd set up outside in the grass. Old folk and country songs blasted from his little portable radio. His workmanship was as impeccable as he was disheveled. The hardest part became convincing him that the bed frames didn't need to be finished with a shiny coat of shellac "for protection" and that they were exactly right as is. He just slow-shrugged and blew a ring of smoke into the air before straddling his motorcycle, revving a couple of times, and speeding off down the country lane in a cloud of sunlit dust.

FILLING IN THE GAPS

Shopping vintage takes time. You can go to a favorite antiques store five times in a row (or more) and not find anything suitable to buy. What you usually save in price, you probably make up for in the legwork and time spent on the hunt for the right piece you need. Most of the time, we love the fun of it. There's no better pastime than a Sunday spent shopping for antiques and having lunch at a country pub. We actually have a storage shed full of things we couldn't pass up because the price was unbeatable, or the item was amazing, but we don't have a proper place for it just yet. But there are times you just need to get a room finished so that it's usable. It's great if you can be of the mind that you'll wait until the perfect piece comes along, but we haven't always been in that position. Foxfire

was busy from the start with guest requests for accommodations, even before the rooms were fully done, and there are basics you need for function, whether it be a lamp, a dresser, a table, or a bench by the door, and sometimes we were lacking those things with the deadline of arriving guests looming. So if we couldn't make it by repurposing something on hand, or find it used in time, we'd shop new so we could get exactly the item we required.

FOXFIRE EVOLVES

As Foxfire transformed and evolved into a space that was open to the public, Tim and I evolved as well. Two major developments happened hot on the heels of each other. The first was our living quarters. At the beginning, Tim and I lived in the cottage while we started renovations on the inn. Then we realized the cottage would bring in extra income for funding the renos if we rented it on Airbnb, so we moved ourselves into the hotel, shifting our bed from one room to the next as the construction work was completed. When guest reservations meant that most of the rooms in the inn were booked, we moved again, this time into an area that was essentially behind the commercial kitchen and part of the staff room. We tacked up a couple of drop cloths to separate where we slept from the staff's desks and chairs. Frequently, a staff member would knock on the wall and abruptly pull back the curtain to ask us a question while we were reading in bed at night. To say there was no work/life separation is an understatement. In a few months, we replaced the drop cloths with an actual wall and added a bathroom to our living area. The privacy felt blissful, even though our whole enclave was only about three hundred square feet. Still, it was progress.

As a homebody, it was a challenge not to be settled into a personal space for two years. We no longer had any possessions of our own. Our furniture and keepsakes had gone into decorating the cottage when we first moved in, and now it was frequently rented out by visiting guests. Everything we owned personally was communal and used by all. On another front, it was also getting harder to recharge ourselves to gain any perspective on future-based decisions when there was no distance whatsoever between us and the property/business. So when a little house in foreclosure came up for sale less than five minutes from Foxfire on a high bank of the rushing Esopus Creek for the unheard-of price of $35,000, we jumped at the chance to buy it. It was a one-level ranch in very poor condition (meaning the ground was visible through a giant hole in the bathroom floor) but we knew we could fix it up.

We were as hands-on remodeling our new cottage—we decided to call it a *cottage* just because it made the small size feel more pleasant—as we were at Foxfire, and we carried our same design-pantry staples into the decor. Starting our design with salvaged vintage items immediately added soul to the space and a sense of history, even though we were rebuilding the house from the studs. ○

Thrifty as we are, we've found that the odd splurge on a beautiful piece, like this rugged low leather chair for the lounge (opposite), or this stunning chandelier (above), elevates all the other furniture in the space. But there's no getting around that a splurge here means a save there, and we still need to compensate by spending less in other areas. That's a task we're always game to take on, since the pride in the luxury item is so worth it.

(opposite) We added vintage windows to the loft and living room, leaving them just as found, chipping paint and all.

(above) We always try to mix function with beauty, considering the details of even basic items like shelves to make sure the wood is a tone we like and the brackets are quality. There is so much good product out there that you don't have to spend a lot, you just have to shop well, relying always on natural materials for authenticity and lasting value.

(opposite) We scoured the Materials section of Craigslist to see what we could find and came across a used glass sunroom for $900. We hatched a plan to add it to the kitchen to expand out our living space and give an incredible view of the fast-flowing river below. The slight catch was that we had to disassemble and remove the sunroom from the seller's house and then figure out how to rebuild it at our place. We did end up with a couple of "leftover pieces" after reassembling that gave me pause, but nevertheless the glass addition is definitely our favorite place to be, day or night, and is now filled with plants, candles, and two comfy armchairs.

(above) A pair of antique stained-glass transom windows we spied in the long grass outside a local antiques barn replaced a boring window over the kitchen sink. A few of the stained-glass panels were broken or missing, so we replaced them with clear amber glass that allowed us to see through to the outside, helping the kitchen not to feel too closed in.

(**opposite**) Bar carts are one of my favorite decor items, and I was so happy to find a wrought-iron one that was compact enough for our little living room. Unlike at Foxfire, where we have to lock alcohol up overnight per the liquor license law, we can just leave the bottles out all the time in our home. Those tiny and picayune lifestyle quirks really strike me after spending so long living on-site, where there was no home/work divide.

(**above**) One difference with decorating our own space is that we can have items that are slightly more fragile than those used in the inn where they would have to withstand hard use. Displays don't get moved around. At the inn, guests will pick up and inspect an item, only to put it back down somewhere else entirely. Sometimes we find things in the strangest places!

As we settled into our cottage, we had just enough distance from Foxfire to step back and look at the overall picture of the business. We were lucky enough to have hired a general manager who was running the day-to-day operations and overseeing the staff—a team of between fifteen and forty people depending on the season of the year—more than capably. Foxfire had grown quickly, and with only fourteen rooms, we were turning away a good many reservation requests each week. The same was true of weddings. We easily filled all the summer and fall weekends with events, and probably could have doubled or tripled that amount if only there were more weekends in any given month, something I lamented often. So the second big evolution was the expansion of Foxfire to include a sister property—beautiful La Colina!

A gorgeous Spanish-style estate, La Colina was built in 1936, and is located on forty-seven rolling acres with incredible long views of black soil farmlands and mountains. It was love at first sight as we were immediately charmed by all the original details: patterned tiles, wrought iron, stucco and plaster walls, beamed ceilings.

There are four guest rooms in the main house, all a pretty good size, one with a balcony (opposite) and one with a view of the pool.

There are four additional guest rooms in an adjoining low building that most recently had been used as sheep sheds. We named those four rooms the cabana rooms, and they were a disaster of wrecked plaster and outdated wiring, but still, they were our favorite of all the rooms because of their potential to be incredibly unique.

There's no doubt the bulk of hard work comes in the middle of any project. Major choices have been made, and there's nothing to do then but settle into the push of labor to get the jobs done. Frustrations and obstacles arise and need to be overcome. Money flows out. Decisions get overwhelming. But every day brings progress, the satisfaction of honest hard work, aching muscles, and a hearty appetite. This part, more than any other, separates the dreamers from the doers. This work is the freefall as your wings are built to fly, and it is what leads to living your dream and not just dreaming it. ○

I had a vision of the cabana rooms looking like a rustic farmhouse you'd be delighted to discover in the countryside in the south of France, with an old-world appeal. We updated the rooms and tiled the showers with handmade clay tiles we found on Craigslist.

DAY

RECIEPS

TIM, EVER RESOURCEFUL, created some of our favorite meals by using what we had on hand while we were knee-deep in the room transformations. He made magic with some empty clay flower pots and an open fire when the kitchen was off-limits after its walls were newly painted.

Flowerpot Spoon Bread

MAKES 1

THE EARLY DAYS at Foxfire required lateral thinking—plank doors on saw-horses became tables, while oven racks and a stack of cinder blocks became grills for the newly uncovered stone fireplace in the lounge. The ancient domestic oven that was in the kitchen when we bought the place had two working settings: on or off. I had a few makeshift wedges that I used to keep the oven door propped open to regulate temperature, so a brick wedged the door open to 350°F (177°C), a cast-iron lid meant 425°F (218°C), and the combo together allowed for slow cooking. There was a noticeable lack of pots and pans too, but we had a plethora of clay flowerpots. So using a cast-iron pot lid to set the oven to the right temperature and a set of clay flowerpots as vessels for baking, our flowerpot spoon bread became a thing.

A homestyle savory cornbread that's closer to a soufflé than bread, we serve this at Foxfire in late summer when the corn is fresh and plentiful. It's completely satisfying as a light lunch with a crisp salad and a glass of tart local cider.

1. Preheat the oven to 425°F (218°C).

2. In a deep bowl, stand the cobs sans kernels upright and drag the knife blade down the cob to "milk" it. Set the liquid aside. This usually yields about 3 tablespoons, but it's just for added flavor, so take what you can get!

3. In a 3-quart heavy saucepan over medium heat, sauté the corn kernels until lightly browned. Add the milk, buttermilk, cornmeal, baking powder, butter, salt, pepper, rosemary leaves, and reserved corn "milk," stir to combine, and bring to a simmer. Stir near constantly until thickened, about 3–4 minutes.

4. Remove from the heat and stir the mixture frequently for 5 minutes until it cools. Whisk in the yolks. Set aside.

5. With a mixer, beat the egg whites with a pinch of salt at medium speed until soft peaks form. Mix a quarter of the whites directly into the corn mixture and then fold in the remaining whites gently throughout.

6. Line a 6-inch terra-cotta flowerpot with parchment paper and spray with nonstick cooking spray. Pour the corn mixture into the pot and set on a baking sheet in the middle rack of the oven. Cook until puffed and golden, about 15 minutes.

7. Serve immediately. The bread will collapse a bit, but the addition of the corn milk and the baking powder helps it keep its structure longer than more traditional methods.

---

2 cups (290 g) fresh-cut corn kernels along with cobs, about 3 ears

1 cup (236 ml) whole milk

1 cup (236 ml) buttermilk

⅓ cup (40 g) coarse whole-grain yellow cornmeal

1 teaspoon baking powder

1 tablespoon unsalted butter

1 teaspoon kosher salt

½ teaspoon white pepper

2 tablespoons fresh rosemary leaves

4 large eggs, separated

Nonstick cooking spray

Camp-Style Trout

TROUT IS TO the Catskills what salmon is to Alaska: a defining food that has made the region famous. The Catskills are the original home of American fly-fishing, and trout is the preeminent fish to catch. There is nothing like the beauty of seeing the anglers out in the fast-moving Esopus Creek in the misty mornings with their lines gracefully arcing out across the water. There are several species of trout in the waters of the Catskills—native brown and brook and introduced speckle and rainbow. All are wonderful to eat and have their own characteristics. Like salmon, a hundred dishes can be made from trout, but the best, as is often the case, is the simplest: I like to roast a whole trout over an open fire with foraged thyme and some local new potatoes. If you are fortunate enough to get brookies for this dish, you may want to cook two per person.

¼ cup (57 g) unsalted butter, softened

1 tablespoon finely chopped garlic

1 tablespoon chopped fresh basil

3–4 small B-size (1½ to 2¼ inch in diameter) potatoes, red or white

¼ cup (65 ml) sunflower or cooking oil

½ cup (65 g) flour

1 teaspoon sea salt

1 teaspoon fresh ground pepper

12–16 ounces fresh trout (rainbow is the easiest to find if buying)

2–3 fresh thyme sprigs

2 peeled whole shallots or 3–4 pearl onions

6–8 grape tomatoes

Half a lemon

1. Combine the butter, garlic, and basil in a small bowl. Spoon the compound butter onto a piece of parchment paper or plastic wrap and roll into a log. Chill in the refrigerator for at least 3 hours before using to allow the flavors to blend.

2. Bring a large pot of salted water to a boil. Add the potatoes and boil until tender but not soft, as they will finish cooking in the cast-iron skillet. Drain and set aside. The potatoes can be cooked in advance.

3. Add the oil to a cast-iron skillet (I use a grill skillet, as I like the marks it leaves) and heat over high heat until the oil starts to shimmer or just smoke.

4. While the oil heats, combine the flour, salt, and ground pepper in a large bowl and dredge the fish in the flour mixture on both sides. Place in the hot oil and cook on one side until the skin is blistered and darkens, about 3–4 minutes.

5. Turn the trout over and move the pan to a cooler spot over the fire, or reduce the heat to medium.

6. Add the thyme sprigs to the top of the fish. Then add the potatoes, shallots, tomatoes, and lemon (flesh side down) to the pan and continue to cook for 5 more minutes. Test the fish for doneness with a thin sharp knife by making a small cut next to the dorsal fin. When the flesh is just turning opaque, it's ready.

7. Lift the fish onto a paper towel–lined dish with a metal spatula and dab away any oil. Be careful not to pull the skin off. Top the fish with a pat of the compound butter and serve with the charred lemon half, potatoes, shallots, and blistered tomatoes.

USE WHAT YOU HAVE 1) Pull the leftover trout meat from the bones and skin, then mix with enough sour cream or Greek yogurt to bind the mixture into a delicious bagel spread. Sprinkle with chopped chives, if desired. **2)** The extra compound butter is great over a steak, and will keep for a good long while in the fridge, so don't worry if you don't use it right away. **3)** If you don't use the fresh thyme right away, leave it out of the fridge to dry, and then strip off and store the leaves for later.

| DIY | # Building a Swedish Torch | WHAT WE LEARNED ALONG THE WAY |

JUST AS SEEING the maker's hand in decor items adds a human element and honors the value of an item that is crafted and made with love, so too does seeing the chef's hand in a delicious dish. Cooking over an open fire has a friendly air of hospitality about it, and guests will often stand close by and chat with Tim as he gets their food ready to serve on one of the bonfire areas or various grills at Foxfire. For a more portable version of this experience, we like to make simple Swedish torches to cook over. Made from a single log, they're an efficient way to cook over a focused flame that's low-maintenance, safe, and fast—perfect for when you're hungry!

Use a dry log that's flat on both ends and is about 2 feet tall. With a chain saw, cut deep slits through the log in a star pattern, stopping each cut a few inches from the bottom so the log holds together as one unit (1+2).

Gather dry sticks of kindling, birch bark, and/or dry grass tinder. Insert a small bunch of kindling into the slits in the center of the log, and then place a larger bunch of kindling and tinder on top of the log and light (3+4).

The embers from the fire on top of the log will drop down into the center of the log and catch the kindling there. Soon the log itself will also catch fire. As air is continually drawn in through the sides, the fire stays ventilated and burning hot. The torch will burn for 2 to 5 hours, plenty of time to cook something tasty like the Fire-Roasted Scallops (page 154). o

STEP-BY-STEP SWEDISH TORCH

Bonfire Oysters

COOKING FOOD OVER an open fire adds a delightful smoky aroma and a perfect amount of char. Could anything be better? We figured that out nearly two million years ago and are still rediscovering it every generation. My own epiphany came when my family acquired our lodge in the hills of New York's Finger Lakes. The cabin had a huge stone fireplace, and, fortunately, the grounds had an old dumping site used by previous owners to toss out mouse-eaten La-Z-Boys and old fridges. In that dump was the remains of a steel side table with legs that fit the rack of one of the abandoned fridges to a T.

I rigged a contraption together and slipped it into the fireplace. I still remember that spring day when I simmered wild gathered ramps, gem-studded puffballs, and small potatoes in a cast-iron pan on the back corner as a freshly caught trout cooked directly on the "grill" off to the side, and a squash gently charred in the embers underneath. Now, whenever I get a fireplace, I devise legs and racks and start cooking.

Oysters roasted over an open flame is one of the first dishes I made at Foxfire. The dish has hints of woodsmoke that marry with the brininess of the oyster and the sharpness of garlic and pecorino. Cultured butter and pancetta add an unctuous finish.

12 oysters

½ cup (113 g) unsalted butter, softened

1 cup (75 g) pecorino Romano, half grated, half shaved

3 garlic cloves, crushed

1 teaspoon Worcestershire sauce

1 tablespoon fresh thyme leaves

4 slices pancetta, cut into thirds

Splash of vermouth or white wine

Coarse sea salt

1. Shuck the oysters and free the oyster from the shell, leaving it resting in the deep bottom half of the shell. Be careful not to pour out the liquid.

2. Mix the butter, grated cheese, garlic, Worcestershire sauce, and thyme into a compound butter. Drop a dab of butter on each oyster, then top each oyster with a piece of pancetta.

3. Place the oysters on a rack over embers or coals (not direct flames). Cover the oysters with a large steel-domed lid or pie pan. Cook for about 2–4 minutes, depending on how hot the fire is, until the pancetta is crisp and the butter compound is melted.

4. Finish with a shaving of cheese, a dash of vermouth or white wine, and a light sprinkle of salt.

Fire-Roasted Scallops with Farro Barley Risotto

SERVES 4

BECAUSE THIS DISH is simple, excellent ingredients and great technique can really shine. When those things are combined, magic happens. This risotto has a nutty flavor and a looser texture that goes so well with roasted scallops.

1. Start a good fire in either the fireplace or on the barbecue. Pat the scallops dry.

2. Cut each bacon strip in half and stretch the bacon with the back end of a chef's knife. Wrap a piece of bacon around each scallop and skewer through with a toothpick to hold it in place.

3. Place the butter in a large pan and melt over medium heat. When the butter starts to sizzle, add the garlic, onions, and basil to the pan and gently brown, about 3 minutes.

4. Add the farro and the barley to the pan, and gently brown the grains until they smell toasted.

5. Add one quarter of the vegetable stock and stir the mixture consistently, adding in more stock a little at a time as it is absorbed. Use as much stock as is needed to cook the risotto until tender and slightly creamy—this will take about 20 minutes. Finish the risotto by stirring in the white wine and seasoning with salt, pepper, and nutmeg to taste.

6. Place a cast-iron pan over the fire and add the oil. When the oil is hot, place the scallops in the pan. Watch the scallops closely, turning frequently to crisp the bacon while still leaving the scallops moist and almost rare at the center.

7. Serve the scallops over the risotto and garnish with basil.

12 fresh or dry-packed u-10 scallops

6 strips of local maple-smoked bacon (see Note)

⅜ cup (170 g) unsalted butter

2 cloves garlic, crushed

½ medium red onion, finely diced

3 sprigs fresh basil, 2 sprigs chopped finely for cooking, 1 for garnish

1 cup (200 g) farro

1 cup (200 g) pearled barley

1½ quarts (14 L) vegetable stock

½ cup (125 ml) dry white wine

1 teaspoon fine sea salt

1 teaspoon white pepper

Pinch of nutmeg, to taste

1 tablespoon olive oil

NOTE: We use Smoke House of the Catskills bacon, but you should try to find your own local bacon for this dish. Avoid using a commercial national-brand bacon if you can help it as it can tend to be wetter and doesn't crisp as nicely.

Pappardelle with Bison Ragu

SERVES 4

THIS IS A perfect weeknight dish since most ingredients can already be found in your pantry and the sauce can cook anywhere from fifteen minutes to over an hour and still taste wonderful. We like to use bison as the protein in this dish, as most often it's organic and pasture-raised.

1. Add the ¼ cup of oil to a large heavy-bottom pot and warm over medium-high heat. Add the onion and cook until it begins to brown, about 3 minutes.

2. Add the bison and sauté until browned. Make sure you're using a pot that's large enough for the meat to spread out. If it's too crowded, the meat may steam and not brown.

3. Add the garlic, carrots, and oregano. Stir to combine.

4. Add all the fresh and canned tomatoes and the tomato paste. Stir and add the whole ancho chili. Reduce the heat to medium and simmer for at least fifteen minutes, and as much as one hour.

5. Stir in the pesto or basil when the sauce is done simmering. Add the salt and pepper to taste and remove and discard the ancho chili.

6. In a separate pot, cook the pappardelle according to the package instructions.

7. Drain the pasta. Toss the pasta in a tablespoon of olive oil and place on a warm serving dish. Top with the bison ragu and grated pecorino and serve with Warm Endive and Artichoke Salad (page 232) and bread for soaking up the delicious sauce.

¼ cup plus 1 tablespoon (80 ml) extra-virgin olive oil

1 medium yellow onion, diced

1 pound ground bison

4 cloves garlic, crushed

1 medium carrot, shredded

2 teaspoons dried oregano

1 pint cherry tomatoes

28-ounce can San Marzano crushed tomatoes

12-ounce can diced tomatoes

16-ounce can tomato paste

1 dried ancho chili

2 tablespoons jarred pesto or ¼ cup (10 g) chopped basil

Kosher salt

Black pepper

1 pound dried pappardelle noodles

Pecorino cheese, grated, for serving

Eggplant with Harissa

SERVES 4

THIS IS A simple preparation for eggplant that utilizes our Foxfire Harissa Spice Powder. It's a variation on a family recipe and gives eggplant a finger-food treatment. Salty, crispy, and spicy, we often serve it as an appetizer before our Lamb Kufta (page 161) along with a great local unfiltered IPA like Sloop Juice Bomb.

1 Italian eggplant

¼ cup (64 g) coarse sea salt, plus more to taste

¼ cup (65 g) olive oil

3 tablespoons Foxfire Harissa Spice Powder (page 98)

1. Cut the whole unpeeled eggplant in half from pole to pole leaving the ends on, then cut the halves into quarters to create wedges that are about 2 inches wide at the bottom.

2. Liberally sprinkle the eggplant with the sea salt and place in a colander in the sink. Allow the eggplant to weep for about 30 minutes. Wipe off the extra salt with a wet paper towel.

3. Brush the wedges with the olive oil and then coat with the harissa spicing to taste.

4. Place the eggplant on an oiled baking sheet under the broiler on a middle rack. Roast until soft and browned on all sides, turning the wedges if needed. (Keep a close eye on the eggplant, as it takes just a few minutes to roast.) When browned and soft, remove from under the heat. Sprinkle with coarse salt to taste and serve warm.

Lamb Kufta

SERVES 4

THIS IS A dish I grew up with and have carried with me everywhere I go. We serve it both in the restaurant and at home when entertaining. Sumac is a unique souring agent that works so well with the richness of lamb. The addition of bulgur acts as bread crumbs do in Italian meatballs, both stretching the lamb and giving it a lighter texture. Because the kufta balls cook quickly in the broth, the onions and parsley inside them stay fresh and offer a wonderful counterbalance to the stewy dish.

1. Boil 1½ cups water. Add the bulgur to a medium-size bowl and pour the boiling water over top and cover. Let stand until cool. If the bulgur did not absorb all the water, strain and let dry.

2. In a small bowl, mix together half the chopped yellow cooking onion, parsley, and pine nuts. Set aside.

3. Place the ground lamb in a large bowl. Mix the cooled bulgur into the lamb by hand, kneading well to incorporate fully. Add 2 cloves of garlic, cumin, cinnamon, and salt to the meat mixture and knead some more.

4. Gather about 2 ounces of meat (golf-ball size, give or take) and form into a ball. Flatten the ball to the size of your hand and place a tablespoon or so of the onion/parsley/pine nuts mixture into the center of the patty. Re-form the ball around the mixture making sure to seal the mix very well. Use some water to help spread the meat mixture to fully enclose the ball. You don't want it to burst open when poached.

5. In a large saucepan with a lid, heat the olive oil over medium heat. Add the remaining yellow onion and garlic, cover, and sweat until soft, about 3 minutes.

6. Add the tomatoes, remaining ½ cup water, a squeeze of lemon, sumac, and coriander seeds. Mix to combine, reduce the heat to low, and steep uncovered for about 10 minutes. The broth should be thin, but flavorful and sour. Taste and add more spicing, if needed.

7. Increase the heat to medium to bring the broth to a very low boil, and add the kufta balls. Put the lid on the pot and cook for five minutes. Keep a close eye on the pot—the sauce should never get to a rolling boil. Turn the balls once and cook for another couple of minutes until firm to the touch.

8. Serve the kufta in a tureen or serving bowl in the broth, sprinkled with chopped green onions and with yogurt on the side to dollop on top of the kufta.

2 cups (500 ml) water

⅔ cup (95 g) dry bulgur wheat

1 medium yellow cooking onion, chopped fine

½ cup (12 g) fresh parsley, coarsely chopped

⅓ cup (45 g) pine nuts

1 pound (454 g) ground lamb

4 cloves garlic, crushed and chopped

2 teaspoons ground cumin

1 teaspoon ground cinnamon

2 teaspoons kosher salt

1 tablespoon olive oil

2 cups (250 g) crushed tomatoes

½ lemon

3 tablespoons ground sumac

2 teaspoons ground coriander seed

3 whole green onions, chopped, for serving

1 cup (250 ml) whole milk yogurt

CHAPTER FOUR

DUSK

REAPING.   IMMERSING.   GATHERING.

ONE OF THE most wonderful things about being outside in nature is how immersive the experience is. All at the same time, every sense is involved, from the breeze touching your hair, to the sound of the birds in the trees and frogs in the pond, to the smell of flowers and fresh-cut grass, to the taste of garden-grown produce, to the beautiful depth of all the layers you see at once from earth to sky. Finessing rooms and adding the finishing touches make up the last layer of the room design, and it's done with the goal of creating a fully immersive sensory experience to complete your design story. Tackling the interior design of your spaces by considering each of the design elements as separate layers—starting with the bones and ending with the finished room—is our way of ensuring that every aspect of the design is given attention, from the macro down to the micro.

This is the time when you'll want to be playfully creative as well as objectively critical. There will be a lot of trying things one way, standing back and studying the result, jumping in to switch things around, then standing back again (and, if you're like me . . . again) until you're satisfied. It's a process I really love because it allows me to indulge all my nitpicky tendencies for a good purpose. The room is your canvas, and you're the artist putting the final brushstrokes on your work. As with a painting, you need to know when to stop and take away anything that starts to feel cluttered or dilutes the impact of another item that would shine if it had proper space around it. I'm often amazed at how an odd little lamp or side chair from the flea market, when given space to be the highlight of a room, can be transformed from an ugly duckling into an artful swan, where suddenly its shape becomes sculptural and authentically charming.

At this point, it can be helpful to take one more photo of the space to literally see the big picture of the room for what's working and what isn't. For me, at least, I can quickly see the space more objectively than when it's three-dimensional in front of me. It's also the way most of us are used to looking at designed rooms—as photos on Pinterest or Instagram. Adding in finishing decor details brings the rooms to life with spirit and personality, and they're the final chapter in the story of your home. No matter what else, this is *your* home and it's the time to please yourself. If you like the way something looks and it makes you feel happy, then your design is successful. Now with these final decorative touches, you'll be able to fully distinguish the style of the room and highlight the vibe you're going after. Down the road as your tastes or trends change, they're easy things to update without having to do any major changes to the bones of the room or the main furnishings. An area rug in the living room, for example, can switch the mood from rustic farmhouse (sisal/jute), to natural (animal hide/sheepskin), to bohemian modern (kilim/Turkish). This is the long-awaited, joyous part when everything comes together. And it's the most fun. The best thing is that you can linger in this phase of choosing the absolute perfect decorative finishes indefinitely while you collect pieces over time or update the decor to correspond with the holidays and seasons. The fun phase lasts the longest, and that's the ultimate reward for all the hard work leading up to it. ○

Rugs and Textiles

LAYERING IN RUGS and textiles softens rooms and breaks up the hard lines of walls and furniture by adding inviting comfort and warmth. They can define areas, add color and pattern, contribute to the mood, and help balance and unify the room's different design elements. We prefer to use natural fibers and materials throughout: jute, sisal, sheepskin, animal hides, wool, linen, cotton. Never say never, but we generally tend to stick to two or three main colors for each room's palette and play with different shades of these colors in our rug selections, since the tones blend and don't add to the busyness. If you have more than one rug in a space, they don't have to match but should complement each other: different patterns are fine, as long as they're in the same relative color range and the scale of the patterns varies between them. If one rug has a large-scale pattern, then the other rug should have a smaller scale pattern so that they don't compete. ○

CATSKILL **FIELD NOTE** MOUNTAINS

FINISHING DETAILS FOR EVERY ROOM

- Rugs
- Textiles and window coverings
- Table and floor lamps
- Mirrors and artwork
- Something made by hand
- Hooks and clothes rails

- Throw pillows and textural elements
- Flowers, branches, greenery, natural curiosities
- Candles (ideally beeswax or soy for a nontoxic burn)
- Music

For the rustic and bohemian styles we prefer, we don't like rugs to visually overwhelm the rest of the space, so you generally won't find us going for bold and showy feature rugs. We like them to add to the overall texture and timeless vibe, so we tend to go with muted old Persian rugs and collect them whenever we see them at a good price. We don't mind if they show wear or if their fringe is a little tattered, but we avoid rugs with any obvious stains or bad smells. In summer months, we'll often take them outside on the grass and heap them with pillows for lounging. We're also a fan of layering rugs, and like the look of cowhide over jute.

| DIY | # Vintage Rug Pillows | WHAT WE LEARNED ALONG THE WAY |

WE'LL COME CLEAN: rugs are an obsession. We've used rugs as tablecloths, furniture covers, wall hangings, tote bags, and to upholster the front of the bar (page 40). We have a collection of vintage rug pillows scattered throughout Foxfire. We pick up old rugs at yard sales and flea markets, and sometimes we use them intact, and sometimes we cut them into smaller pieces. If the rugs have finished edges all around, you can just fold them together to create a seam down the middle. Then, you just blanket stitch the seam and two sides together using cotton cord and an embroidery needle. Vintage silk scarves also make great pillows, and we've been known to cut up skirts and dresses in fabrics we like from thrift stores and turn those into pillows too!

YOU'LL NEED

- Rug remnant
- Cotton canvas fabric, for backing
- Sewing machine (optional)
- Embroidery needle and cotton cord
- Fiberfill

1. Decide how big you want to make your pillow based on the rug's pattern.

2. Cut your rug down to the size you want for your pillow front with one extra inch all around to account for the seam and any fraying. Cut the backing fabric to the same size. Lay the two fabrics on top of each other with the design-side of the fabrics facing in.

3. If you have a sewing machine with a needle that can accommodate the thickness of the rug, sew together the fabric on three sides, leaving a 1-inch seam all around. Begin stitching up the fourth side, stopping when a large enough space to get your hand in to stuff the pillow and comfortably turn it right side out remains. (We hand-sew the pillows since we only have an inherited antique sewing machine that's not up to the task.)

4. Stuff the pillow with fiberfill and hand stitch the opening closed. ○

Velvet banquettes in the dining room are covered with natural sheepskin rugs for cushy comfort. We love the mix of the raspberry velvet with the creamy white of the sheepskins, and the contrast in the textures goes with our rustic-glam vibe. We also like to use thin cotton rugs that drape nicely, Indian block-print rugs or sheepskins, as cushion covers on settees and love seats. This is a great option if you have kids or pets and want some protection for your upholstery.

(**opposite**) Textiles are amazing for adding fresh color to a room and for unifying the different elements. Whenever we come across them, we collect beautiful old curtain panels, saris, blankets, tablecloths, you name it, because we always find a place for them, even if they're just folded in a basket on the floor. We drape richly colored vintage indigos over the backs of some of the dining room chairs or accent tables to add a layer of interest. Different patterns and textures will create different moods. We're dying to try out some faded vintage chintz in the summer.

(**above**) We regularly drape fabric pieces, scarves, and throw blankets over surfaces to add layers for interest but also to stimulate touch. Old cotton lace and crocheted pieces can make lovely curtains that still let the light filter in.

(opposite) Window coverings can be costly. I had purchased a collection of vintage silk saris in muted pinks, greens, and lilacs from a local antiques store at a good price thinking I'd use them as gorgeous tablecloths for a special event, but then I could never bring myself to lay them out knowing they'd be ruined after just one use with the inevitable spills of food and wine. So instead I sewed the gauzy, ethereal sari fabric into window coverings for the lounge. The prints add an eclectic vibe, plus they were really easy to make. Essentially, they're just rectangles measured to fit the windows, with a channel at the top for a café rod, and French seams for the other three sides. Simple woven blinds underneath help shade the room further from the sun that floods in brilliantly in the afternoons.

(above) Woven wood and bamboo blinds are our regular go-to and have been since my college days. They just have a nice rustic simplicity that works in any style of space.

Lighting

ALL OF THESE last layers of the room decor accentuate the design style you're creating, and your choices of floor and table lamps are key to that. We like rooms to have a mix of overhead lighting, wall sconces and pendants, table lamps, and floor lamps, but if you can swing at least two to three of those options, you'll be in good shape. Light coming from varying height sources disperses the light most evenly throughout the room. The types of lampshades you choose can quickly define a style too. In general, the smoother and more luxurious the material (think silk or velvet), the more upscale and modern the room, while rougher materials (think burlap or wicker) tend to go with more rustic, country-style decors. I would have a ton of lamps in every room—if it wouldn't look bizarre—because they're just so sculptural and provide a winning blend of beauty and practicality. The only rules of thumb we keep in mind are to have table lamps shine at eye level so you're not looking at the top or bottom of the bulb, and to be sure to have a mix of ambient and directional light so your rooms will be multifunctional. **o**

This floor lamp gets moved around a lot, but we like that it holds its own wherever it lands. It's a gorgeous pale green onyx and antique brass, so sculptural against the gray walls. We have a flexibly imposed house rule that we don't spend more than $125 for a floor lamp. This one was $85 in a local antiques shop, so it came home with us.

(opposite, top) These pretty tangerine-colored lamps pop against the pale ochre plaster walls. We were immediately drawn to the tightly woven burlap shades that have the same tangerine interiors as the lamp bases. The glow at night is beyond lovely, as the whole room takes on a warm hue.

(opposite, bottom) The bedrooms at La Colina feature ceramic pendant lights we commissioned from local potters located near Foxfire. We love the smooth, simple shapes of the pendants, as well as the gentle ambient glow they cast. The organic imperfections in the glaze are entirely harmonious with the rugged plaster walls and concrete floors of the cabana rooms and together create a haven of tranquility.

Wall Hangings, Mirrors, and Artisanal Details

ARTWORK IS SO entirely personal, and it's one of the best ways to put your final signature on a room and create a mood. We're always on the lookout for vintage art, since it's as good when blended into a new room as it is in a more antique space. We love old oil portraits even if they're a little ragged and the paint is somewhat chipped. Seascapes and botanicals are our go-tos, but we stay open to everything, since you never know what you'll find. Vintage fabrics or rugs hung on the walls are another good way to showcase thrifted finds, and we use a lot of antique mirrors in our designs because not only do they bounce the light and make spaces brighter, especially if used strategically by windows, but also the frames function as art when they're ornate or beautifully shaped. If the mirror is dulled with age, it can still add a little glimmer when placed above a table with a lamp or candle on it, plus it has a faded beauty all its own. The mix of old and new wonderfully gives a room soul. The same is true for artisanal details. Pieces that show the maker's hand add a sense of humanity since they're usually not perfect, whether it's a drip in the ceramic glaze of a vessel or a painting with a slightly wonky perspective. These "flaws" in old and handmade items create homey comfort and round out the look of regular store-bought furnishings so rooms look as though they've evolved over time and are both current and ageless in style. **o**

(opposite) We're always on the lookout for portraits when we go antiquing. A painting of a person instantly adds the warmth of company to a bare wall. That said, we like to choose portraits the way we would choose people we want to spend time with, so we often turn away from those with brooding or morose expressions and instead opt for portraits like this young woman who we come to consider friends and familiar parts of the household. In this portrait, the brown paint of the woman's hair has crumbled off over the years, resulting in a mottled patina that looks like salon highlights if you stand back far enough.

(above) With vintage art, we don't worry if there's a rip in the canvas or chipped paint because it adds a nice, lived-in touch. Unframed canvases are often less expensive, and have a simple, humble quality to them that's really appealing.

(opposite) I'm a collector at heart and go through phases of what I like to collect at any given time, from vintage silver-plated ice buckets to old bottles to roe antlers to pottery to who knows what will catch my eye next. Grouping collections is the best way to give them design impact and keep them from looking cluttered.

(above) We were lucky enough to have the team from Fort Lonesome in Austin, Texas, stitch our logo (created by the equally talented LAND design crew) onto a vintage indigo textile. Handmade items are imbued with the care of the maker. More and more, as modern living becomes about instant news and information, fast food, and immediate communications, the value of something made personally by hand, taking hours or weeks or even years to complete, becomes even more precious. The items don't have to be overly expensive to have a richness that is worth more than money can buy. Our favorite rooms always have something handmade in them.

(opposite and above) I'm not sure exactly when our passion for hooks started, but now they're part of all the bedrooms we set up. Sure, guests can heap their clothes on a chair in the corner but it's so much nicer to hang them on a hook. Plus, the hook rails add a nice bit of architecture to the rooms as well. Whenever we unearth hand-forged iron hooks or rustic wood clothes rails at flea markets, we pick them up knowing we'll use them somewhere, sometime.

Throw Pillows and Texture

THERE'S NOTHING BETTER than a squishy pillow when you want to relax. All shapes, sizes, and styles will work to layer interesting texture and color into a space. Pillows reconcile the design features so that everything looks unified and thoughtfully put together, not to mention that they add softness and interest to the structural look of the furniture. Pillows can play off or highlight colors that are in artwork and furnishings and echo that color in another part of the room. We often use solid-color velvet pillows as a base because you can find them in the most beautiful shades, including the dusky off-tone pinks, blues, greens, and grays that we tend to love, then we mix and match from there. Options abound. You can use a variety of pillows in the same color family, two or three complementary colors, different patterns and prints (just keep the scale similar)— really it's hard not to be smitten with pillows in general. They're affordable, pretty, and practical, which is a winning trifecta. **o**

If you want to take a design risk or step outside your comfort zone, pillows are a good place to do that. While I may not want an entire floral armchair, I can add a chintz pillow to a neutral linen chair and get a taste of the same effect. The same is true for a shaggy, sequined Moroccan pillow or any bold pattern. Pillows let a little go a long way. You can try out a new color and date it for a while before you commit to marrying it by bringing in a larger piece. From a budget point of view, it's also a good way to showcase an expensive fabric you've fallen in love with, since the yard you'd need to make a pillow might be in reach, whereas a whole upholstered sofa's worth is not.

Bringing Nature In

EVERY SPACE WE decorate has found and foraged treasures from nature. These are staple ingredients added into the rooms to give a sense of wonder and life. They are a way of preserving a moment in time that was once full and ripe and splendid and letting us interact with the natural world, even when indoors.

Natural curiosities are probably the design passion I've carried with me the longest. I can't think of any room I've ever lived in that hasn't had a found treasure, whether it's a shell or coral washed up from the sea, shed antlers or lichen found in the woods, or flowers picked from the meadow. Bringing nature inside for its wonder and beauty is vital to my sense of place and connection to the world, so it's lucky that the gardens at Foxfire are an ever-changing source of greenery and florals that we gather to bring inside every few days. We deliberately keep rooms pared down and somewhat neutral to leave space for the wildness of flowers, branches, and plants. We prefer arrangements to be loose and unfussy and reflect the natural environment they came from. Both at Foxfire and La Colina, no room is complete without the life that flowers give it, and so we have casual arrangements in every space. ○

(above) At La Colina, eucalyptus leaves tied in the shower release their fresh minty scent as the hot water flows for some soothing aromatherapy.

(opposite) Often, we'll use just one or two types of flowers in a vase, rather than a whole mishmash of competing flowers.

(opposite and left) For vessels, we love pottery, metals like brass and silver that have darkened with the passage of time, vintage bottles or jars, and weathered urns.

(above) We often add foraged greenery and seasonal flowers cut from the gardens to enliven the spaces inside, even when all the windows allow for surrounding green views.

(page 196) Dried flowers have gotten a bad rap thanks to some peculiar potpourris and the fact that some people hold on to them until they're faded and dusty. Nothing lasts forever! Used judiciously, though, a few sprigs of dried lavender or a marigold chain left over from a wedding can add a pretty dash of color for a few months before needing to be replaced.

(page 197) One of our favorite things to do is match the flowers to the color of the vase or the wall background because that highlights and reinforces the colors of the flowers themselves even more.

<table>
<tr><td>**DIY**</td><td># Making a Wild Floral Arrangement</td><td>**WHAT WE LEARNED ALONG THE WAY**</td></tr>
</table>

A NATURAL LUXURY, flowers in a room have been proven to elevate mood and improve emotional health. Here are some of our tips for making a loose, nature-inspired arrangement that will make you happy.

YOU'LL NEED

- An assortment of wildflowers and greenery

- Sharp knife

- Unique vessels

- Flower frogs of varying sizes

1. Gather the florals you'll be using and trim the ends with a sharp knife. We like to choose stems or branches that already have bends and curves that will complement the straighter stems. Not everything has to have leaves or flowers, or be perfect. A leaf with a curl or browning, or maybe a few holes from a hungry caterpillar, can be charming and just plain real. A mix of drooping greens and flowing vines can be foraged and added to the flowers to echo the wildness found in nature. The flowers should look only slightly more ordered than what you'd find growing in the garden.

2. Keep the flowers in water while you work. Warm water will help to open closed blooms, while cold water tends to slow the blooming process.

3. Choose a vessel that will suit your selection of flowers. The key is to think about the size of the vessel's opening; the wider it is, the more flowers you'll need. The vessel shouldn't dominate the arrangement or overshadow the flowers, so plan to make an arrangement that's one and a half times as high as the vessel and equally as wide.

4. Flower frogs are worth collecting in different sizes to put at the bottom of your vases. The grid openings or spikes in the frog help the flowers to stay in place in the vessel as you make the arrangement.

5. Create the base and greenery first. Nature isn't symmetrical, so neither should the arrangement be. Have an arching vine flow out to one side, even long enough to fall across the table, or high above the vessel. As you work, hold each stem or branch up in front of you and study its natural shape and movement before adding it to the vessel so you're not forcing it to do what it wasn't made to do. Trim any leaves that will fall below the surface of the water, as well as any leaves that don't let the branch or flower shine. Rarely do we put a stem in a vase without carefully cutting off quite a few leaves, and even some flowers, to let the others show their shape. You never want to have too many leaves bunched into the opening of the vessel. The entire arrangement should have an airiness and space to see through the flowers. We always try to a hide some of the vessel's opening with greenery for a less stark look.

6. Think about a focal point for the display. Cluster flowers more profusely on one side than the other so that your eye has a place to land before sweeping across to take in the whole arrangement. If there's a blend of dark and light flowers, try to transition across the arrangement like an ombré effect, moving from darker shades to lighter.

7. Turn the arrangement as you work, or step around it so you can see it from all sides if it will be placed in the center of a table. Every side should be beautiful in its own way. ○

The winter doesn't stop us from foraging dried grasses that are beautifully textural and sculptural. We actually love them so much that we often keep the juxtaposition of dried grasses with freshly cut flowers all year long. Wintery green pine boughs adorn the chandelier in the colder months and give the space much-needed life and a romantic ambience.

(opposite, above, and below) For us, nature is always at the center of everything, whether it's considering how sunlight enters the rooms, or using earthy natural materials like iron, leather, linen, concrete, woven grasses, and wood in the decor.

(right, top and bottom) Another aspect of nature we use selectively as a way to celebrate the natural world is taxidermy. It may not be for everyone, but for us it's another method of blurring the lines between outdoors and in, wild and tame.

(opposite and above) Antlers and horns can function as sculpture. They add not only texture to a space but also a dynamism that comes from being three-dimensional rather than flat like a mirror or painting. Though their popularity may flare and fade with decorating trends, they remain timeless to us in the same way a beautiful piece of coral or an iridescent feather remains endlessly appealing and worthy of display.

Scent and Sound

STYLING THE ROOMS by layering in the finishing touches ensures that when guests come to Foxfire, they can be fully immersed in the setting and enjoy a complete body and soul getaway from their day-to-day lives. A full sensory experience is what hospitality and successful design are all about, whether in your home, or at a "home away from home" like Foxfire strives to be. Early on, we knew that we wanted to have a signature scent for the inn just as people have a signature fragrance they wear. We were lucky to discover a wonderful Brooklyn-based fragrance company called Cavern New York that makes quality scented products by hand in small batches. We worked with Cavern to develop a scent that felt right to us, sampling essential oil mixes in tiny bottles until we hit on a combination we adored. Made with 100 percent American-grown soy wax, "Sundown" is the most intoxicating and memorable blend of sage, bitter orange, ivy, teakwood, orris, and frankincense. We burn the candles in the public spaces at Foxfire, and we sell them at the inn and online as well. The fragrance has been so popular with our guests that we created a roll-on perfume version that anyone can wear. For variety, we created a second, lighter scent called "Kismet" that's a blend of orange blossom, lemon verbena, neroli, mandarin, galbanum, Ravensara, and black pepper. Just listing the ingredients sounds divine. La Colina has its own signature scent now, too (appropriately called "La Colina," also developed with Cavern), that's a sultry blend of saffron, cypress, thyme, incense, vanilla bean, and rose. They're all uniquely amazing, and we couldn't be happier with the moods they help create.

Along with scent for setting a welcoming vibe, music is right up there for making the whole space feel inviting. We have assorted playlists for various times of the day and different situations. We call on an amazing DJ, Matt Cully, to make the playlists for us, and we have a pretty great collection of them now that are accessible on Spotify. Hosting for us is about curating an experience that's subtle but intuitively recognized as something special by our guests. We're humbled by how often people come into Foxfire and right away say that it feels magical. That *magic* is the alchemy of all the senses being captivated at once with care and creativity. Once the music is playing, we're ready to open the doors wide, pour some drinks, including our delicious white sangria, and embrace being a gathering place for travelers and locals alike. ○

CATSKILL **FIELD NOTE** MOUNTAINS

"DUSK" PLAYLIST BY MATT CULLY

"Journey in Satchidananda"..............................Alice Coltrane, featuring Pharoah Sanders
"Essence of Sapphire"..Dorothy Ashby
"Collage"...The Three Degrees
"When the Lights are Low"...The Paragons
"Our Love"...The Edge of Daybreak
"County Line"..Cass McCombs
"Windows"..Sugar Candy Mountain
"I Am the Changer"...Cotton Jones
"Caboclo"..Arthur Verocai
"Satellite of Love"..Lou Reed
"I Believe to My Soul"..Ray Charles
"Night Time"..Kevin Morby

RECIPES

AT ITS CORE, a room's finishing touches act as a welcome to new guests in the same way that sharing delicious food and drinks brings people together. We like to serve meals family style in large bowls or platters, as it quickly unites everyone at the table and adds to the warmth of good company. On sunny days, we take this ethos outdoors, often packing picnic baskets for our guests to take on hikes or to enjoy on the property. Either way, flowers and candles are a must to add to the feast for your eyes, as are endless bottles of wine.

Foxfire's White Sangria

THIS SANGRIA SHOULD look as delicious as it tastes. Make sure to find an attractive glass drink dispenser or large pitcher to serve it.

Add all ingredients to your serving container and stir to combine. Refrigerate for at least an hour before serving.

1 bottle Entre-Deux-Mers white wine

6 ounces pear liqueur

2 ounces citrus vodka

12 ounces club soda

1 pint fresh strawberries, sliced

1 pint fresh blueberries

½ lemon, sliced thinly

3 sprigs of thyme

¼ cup (13 g) mint leaves

TIPS FOR PACKING A PICNIC

Picnics are one of life's happiest activities. We often pack picnic baskets for our guests to take on hikes or to enjoy on the property, and Tim and I personally like to celebrate our special occasions like anniversaries and birthdays with picnics in some of our favorite locations.

- Use lock-top containers for everything—don't trust that deli counter lids will stay on or not leak.

- Charcuterie is the best food for a picnic. Bring along a small wooden cutting board. It's handy for cutting and serving cheeses and salamis since the ground may not be even.

- Boxed wine and sturdy tumblers. Enough said.

- Pack any dressings or condiments in separate containers, or bring mini-size versions, and add them right before you're about to eat to prevent soggy sandwiches or salads. The less you have to take home, the better.

- Bring lots of cutlery since there probably won't be anywhere to rinse it off. We put any used cutlery in a ziplock bag to bring home.

- Use eco-friendly disposable plates.

- Wet naps and napkins make for easy cleanup.

- Line the bottom of your cooler with freezer packs, and then layer in the food in the reverse order you expect to eat it, so your first course is at the top. Frozen water bottles on top serve a dual purpose of keeping the food cool and making sure you stay hydrated.

- Pack a trash bag in case public cans are not easily accessible.

Rustic Tortilla Pie

THIS IS A time-consuming dish with a long list of ingredients, but the hours of slow cooking will be worth it. Be brave, my new friend, and embrace the journey, because the ends will justify the means, and glory is at hand. This rustic, layered dish is comfort food at its best.

1. **MAKE THE PORK BUTT.** Preheat the oven to 225°F (107°C). Rub the butt with salt, 1 tablespoon garlic, and half the cumin, oregano, and white pepper.

2. Mix the remaining portions of cumin, oregano, white pepper with the chilies, lime juice, orange juice, 6 tablespoons olive oil, and 1 heaping tablespoon garlic together to form a marinade.

3. In a heavy cast-iron pot or Dutch oven, heat the remaining 2 tablespoons oil over medium heat. Add the roast and brown on all sides.

4. Pour the marinade over the meat and cook covered with foil for 3–4 hours, until the meat falls from the bone.

5. Remove the roast and reserve any liquid that is left. Let cool, then skim the fat from the liquid and set both the liquid and the fat aside. Save the pork fat in the fridge as it will keep for several weeks and can be used in refried beans (I elected not to use it in this recipe), or in savory pie crusts or biscuits.

6. **MAKE THE REFRIED BEANS.** Add the oil to a pressure cooker pot without the lid and heat over medium heat (or if you're using an electric, medium-high heat). Add the onion, garlic, chamomile, and cilantro, and cook until the onions start to brown, about 4–5 minutes.

7. Add the beans, ancho chili, water, broth, and stout. Stir to combine, cover, and lock the pot lid. Cook for 35 minutes.

8. Turn off the burner or the pot and allow natural pressure release. This helps the beans absorb more flavor. Check a bean; it should be tender. If it's not, bring back to a simmer and cook until tender. Carefully remove the cover and drain the liquid from the beans, reserving a few cups of liquid. Set the liquid aside.

9. Return the beans to the pot. Add the salt and about ½ cup of the reserved liquid. Use a wooden spoon and stir the beans vigorously to start breaking them down. You're looking for a final texture that is creamy, slightly stiff, and contains many bean chunks but has few if any whole beans left. The mixture needs to be relatively thick. If they need more liquid, add a very little at a time until you reach your desired consistency.

10. Taste and adjust the salt. Let the beans cool and stiffen. They should be at least as thick as peanut butter when cool.

11. **MAKE THE YELLOW RICE.** In a medium-size heavy-bottom pot, heat the oil over medium heat and add the rice. Cook until the rice starts to brown, about 2 minutes.

FOR THE PORK

1 medium Boston butt, approximately 4 pounds

1½ teaspoons kosher salt

6 garlic cloves, pressed or finely chopped

1 tablespoon ground cumin

1 tablespoon dried oregano

2 teaspoons white pepper

3 dried whole ancho chilies, 2 rehydrated and chopped fine

½ cup (125 ml) fresh lime juice

½ cup (125 ml) fresh orange juice

½ cup (125 ml) olive oil

¼ cup (12 g) chopped cilantro or amount to taste, for assembly

½ small white onion, chopped, for assembly

FOR THE REFRIED BEANS

1 cup (250 ml) vegetable oil or olive oil

1 small white onion, diced

1 clove garlic, chopped

1 teaspoon chamomile

2 tablespoons chopped cilantro

½ pound dried pinto beans

1 ancho chili

2 cups (500 ml) water

1 cup (250 ml) pork broth from the Boston butt (can substitute chicken broth, if needed)

1 cup flat stout or porter

1 teaspoon kosher salt

½ cup cotija (60 g) or feta cheese (75 g), for assembly

CONTINUES

12. Add the onions and cook for 2 minutes. Add the garlic and cook until fragrant, about 1 minute.

13. Pour about 1½ cups of the pork broth from step 5 into the rice mixture and bring to a boil. Stir in the tomato paste, turmeric, cumin, sofrito, salt, and black pepper into the broth and return to a boil. Cover, reduce the heat to low, and simmer until the rice is cooked and firm, but not watery, about 15–20 minutes.

14. Stir the peas and carrots into the cooked rice. Set aside.

15. **MAKE THE TORTILLAS.** In the bowl of a stand mixer with the dough hook attachment, combine the flours, salt, and baking powder and mix until well combined.

16. With the mixer running at medium speed, add the oil and water slowly. After about a minute, the mixture will come together to form a ball. Decrease the mixing speed to low and continue to mix for another minute until the dough is smooth and has a bit of a sheen.

17. Transfer the dough to a well-floured work surface. Divide into eight equal portions.

18. Coat each ball with flour and flatten with the palm of your hand. Cover the flattened balls of dough with a clean kitchen towel and allow to rest for at least 20 minutes.

19. On a well-floured work surface, roll each dough piece into a rough circle, about 8–10 inches in diameter.

20. Heat a large pan over medium heat. When the pan is hot, place one dough circle into the pan and allow to cook about a minute or until the bottom has just started to brown. The top side should have a few bubbles. If the tortillas are browning too fast, reduce the heat a little. Conversely, if it's taking longer than a minute to get brown spots on the underside of the tortillas, increase the heat a tad. Flip to the other side and cook for 15–20 seconds. The tortillas should be nice and soft but have a few small brown spots on the surface. Remove from the pan with tongs and stack in a covered container or with a towel over the plate to keep the tortillas soft.

21. **FINISH COOKING AND ASSEMBLE THE PIE.** Preheat the oven to 350°F (177°C). Oil the inside of a 6–8-quart cast-iron pot or enamel casserole pot very well.

22. Place a tortilla on the bottom of the pot. The tortilla should climb the sides to about a third of the way up. Cut two tortillas in half to finish lining the sides of the pot.

23. Put a layer of refried beans about a third of the way up the pot on the bottom. Cover with a tortilla. Add a layer of rice the same thickness as the beans. Sprinkle the cotija or feta cheese over the rice. Cover with another tortilla.

24. Add the pork mixture. Cover with a tortilla. As the pot flares out, this layer may need two tortillas to cover. Lightly oil the top tortillas so they brown and do not stick to the pot lid.

FOR THE YELLOW RICE

3 tablespoons vegetable oil

¾ cup jasmine rice (145 g) or basmati rice (135 g), well rinsed

¼ cup (35 g) finely chopped onion

2 garlic cloves, chopped

1½ cups (375 ml) pork broth from the Boston butt (can substitute chicken broth, if needed)

1 tablespoon tomato paste

1 teaspoon turmeric

1 teaspoon cumin

1 tablespoon sofrito or tomato salsa

1 teaspoon fine sea salt

1 teaspoon black pepper

½ cup (43 g) frozen peas and carrots

FOR THE TORTILLAS

1 cup (125 g) all-purpose flour

½ cup (65 g) masa harina

1 teaspoon salt

¾ teaspoon baking powder

1 tablespoon vegetable oil

½ cup (125 ml) warm water

FOR THE ACCOMPANIMENTS

Hot sauces

Salsas

Limes

Grated sharp cheddar cheese

Fresh cilantro sprigs

DUSK

RUSTIC TORTILLA PIE, CONTINUED

25. Cover and place in the oven for about 30 minutes. Since all the ingredients are already cooked, you're just looking to heat the dish through and crisp the tortillas.

26. Remove the dish from the oven and let cool for 5 minutes with the lid off. Run a thin flexible blade around the pot and as far under as possible to release anything that's stuck. Place a large plate on top of the pot and carefully turn the pot upside down onto the plate and give a firm shake in one smooth motion to release the pie onto the plate. Let cool further to make slicing easier.

27. Serve with a selection of hot sauces, salsas, and if you like, sour cream and grated sharp cheddar cheese.

Venison Kielbasa Potjie

SERVES 8

POTJIE IS A traditional backyard barbecue dish of South Africa that I learned about from my stepfather and have enjoyed many times with wine-making friends from Stellenbosch. Traditionally, a potjie pot is a version of a cast-iron Dutch oven with legs. A small fire is kept underneath the pot to slow-cook the potjie (see Note). Everybody there seems to have their own special take on this dish, but the mark of a true potjiekos chef is in the layering and then the listening. Once the dish is set, the lid remains closed until it's finished, so a potjiekos chef must listen to the potjie pot "talk" to know when it's done without burning or overcooking it. The best accompaniments to this dish are a loaf of French bread and a bottle of Pinotage or crisp lager.

1. Heat the pot and add the meat and onions. Dry-cook, stirring constantly until they are browned, about 5 minutes.

2. Sprinkle in a third of the caraway seeds and fennel seeds, and add a sprig of thyme.

3. Begin the layering process. Layer in the carrots, then the tomatoes, fennel, and green pepper. Add another third of the caraway seeds and fennel seeds, and another sprig of thyme.

4. Finish layering the potjie with the new potatoes, and the remainder of the caraway seeds, fennel seeds, and thyme sprigs. Pour the beer over the potjie and put the lid on the pot.

5. Listen to the bubbling in the pot—it should sound like a stew cooking. If the bubbling stops and there is sizzling, move the pot off the heat. The reason for not removing the lid is to keep the heat in and cook the stew quicker. However, if you're not sure of how things are going, take a peek. Use a spoon to work to the bottom of the pot to see if anything is sticking. If the stew is too dry, add more beer; if too wet, cook for a bit with the lid off. The dish is done when the potatoes are fully cooked and soft, about 45 minutes to an hour.

6. Now for the nontraditional move. Once the potjie is done, I give it an easy toss to distribute the rich juices from the bottom throughout the pot.

USE WHAT YOU HAVE A great use for leftover potjie is a morning frittata. Use tongs to remove the pieces from the liquid. Chop the potjie pieces into medium chunks and sauté in olive oil in a 9-inch cast-iron pan to heat through. Beat 6 eggs and ¼ cup buttermilk together, then add salt, pepper, and nutmeg to taste. Pour the egg mixture in the hot pan and place in a 325°F (163°C) oven until set, about 15 minutes.

2 pounds smoked venison kielbasa, sliced

1 large Vidalia onion, sliced

1 tablespoon caraway seeds

1 tablespoon fennel seeds

8 sprigs thyme

1 to 2 each white, purple, and yellow heirloom carrots, depending on size, cut into ¾ pieces on the bias

1 pint cherry tomatoes

1 fennel bulb, chopped

1 large green pepper, cubed

8 B-size (1½ to 2¼ inch in diameter) new potatoes, whole

1¼ cups (315 ml) pilsner beer

NOTE: For this recipe, I used a traditional cast-iron pot that I hung from a tripod over an open fire. A barbecue grill can be used as well; just be sure the fire is hot. If you do not have a grill, you can cook this in the oven at 325°F (163°C) for about 45 minutes.

Family-Style Kimchi Smoked Lamb

SERVES 8

THIS IS A great stay-at-home weekend dish to make in a smoker or on the grill. Get the fire going around noon and let the wood reduce to embers while you putter around the garden or enjoy some R & R in other ways. Over the next 4 to 5 hours, add the lamb and casually keep an eye on the fire, adding small bits of soaked wood while you enjoy the rich hickory-scented smoke wafting through your yard and revving up your appetite.

Because lamb has such a pronounced flavor, it's a good base for exploring new and creative flavor profiles without overwhelming the meat. Here, its natural flavor is enhanced by the slight heat and spiciness of the cinnamon and the pungency of the kimchi. The combination creates a deep, full profile reminiscent of both a Southern pit barbecue and an African stew. We like to serve it with a black rice and lime risotto, and braised bok choy or kale sauté.

1. Ready a smoker or charcoal grill barbecue. Start a small wood fire in the barbecue. Let the wood burn down to a good ember bed. This may take an hour or more. Add medium-size pieces of wood until the embers are hot and fill about a third of the barbecue. You can use hardwood charcoal at this point to keep a strong ember bed going. Once the ember bed is ready and you've prepared the lamb, start adding the soaked wood chips.

2. Strain the kimchi and reserve the liquid. In a blender, mix the strained kimchi, gochujang, a quarter of the cinnamon, and sesame oil to make a thick paste. Use the reserved kimchi liquid to thin the paste if it's too thick.

3. Butterfly the leg of lamb and rub the outside of the flesh with the sea salt. Then rub the inside with the paste, making sure to reserve enough to coat the outside too.

4. Close and retie the leg of lamb. Rub the outside with the paste, then coat the whole leg with the remaining cinnamon powder.

5. When the ember bed is ready (hot with no flames and smoke coming from the soaked chips), place the lamb on a rack off to one side so it isn't directly over the heat.

6. Cook the lamb for 4–5 hours, rotating often. The trick is to create a firm bark (the crisp but not scorched outside of the meat). The paste will keep the inside slightly red even when the meat is cooked through. I like the roast to pull apart using a gentle tug with a fork, leaving just enough structure left to slice, but you can cook it longer or shorter depending on preference.

7. When the roast is done, set aside to rest for at least 15 or up to 30 minutes.

8. Quarter and core the pears and place them on the grill beside the whole peppers. Let the pears and peppers cook over the remaining embers for about 15 minutes as the roast rests. Serve together and enjoy.

3–4 pieces of 2-inch-wide hardwood to create an ember bed

Hardwood charcoal

2–3 pounds of soaked hickory or mesquite wood chips for smoking

1 cup Quick Simple Kimchi (page 109)

1–2 tablespoons gochujang to taste

1 cup (132 g) cinnamon

1 tablespoon toasted sesame oil

5–7 pound boneless leg of lamb

2 tablespoons fine sea salt

4 Bartlett or Asian pears

16 sweet mini red peppers

USE WHAT YOU HAVE
This leftover lamb makes a great banh mi–style sandwich when chopped and served on a hard roll with sliced radish, cilantro, and mayo.

Coq Au Cidre

SERVES 4

THE CATSKILLS/HUDSON valley region is quickly becoming a world-renowned pomicultural (fruit-growing) area that produces some of the best hard ciders found anywhere, especially Normandy-style dry and sour ciders. This type of cider combines perfectly with the sweetness of local wild apples, damson prune plums, and flavorful free-range chicken.

1. Pat the chicken pieces dry and season with salt and white pepper.

2. In a large bowl, marinate the chicken in 1½ cups cider while preparing the remainder of the dish. Reserve this liquid.

3. Add the flour to a large bowl and season with 1 teaspoon each salt and white pepper, and a pinch of nutmeg. Whisk to combine and set aside.

4. Heat the oven to 350°F (177°C). Remove the chicken from the cider and pat dry again, reserving the cider. Dredge the chicken in the seasoned flour.

5. Add the grapeseed oil to a large cast-iron or stainless steel oven-safe pan, and brown the chicken pieces over medium-high heat. Do three or four pieces at a time so as not to crowd the chicken. Remove from the pan and set aside. Keep the pan over the heat.

6. Deglaze the pan by adding ½ cup of cider and scraping up the browned bits from the bottom. Add the onions and potatoes to the pan, then layer the apples and plums, and top with the chicken. Toss in the thyme sprigs.

7. Add another ½ cup of the reserved cider, cover the pan with foil, and place in the oven. Cook for about 45 minutes, or until the chicken is cooked through. When done, the chicken should have about ¾ cup of reduced cider sauce thickened from the dredging flour. If the dish loses too much liquid while cooking, add some more cider.

8. Drizzle the liquid over and serve on a warm platter.

USE WHAT YOU HAVE The leftovers from this dish make great chicken noodle soup the next day. Shred the chicken, boil egg noodles, use a good-quality chicken stock, and add sautéed celery and the apples and plums.

Whole free-range organic chicken, cut into 8 pieces

2 teaspoons kosher salt

2 teaspoons white pepper

2 cups (500 ml) dry cider (use your local cider if there is one, even if it's not bone-dry)

½ cup (65 g) all-purpose flour

Pinch of nutmeg

2 tablespoons grapeseed or other neutral cooking oil

2 medium yellow onions, peeled and cut into sixths

8 small whole white potatoes

2 cooking apples, such as McIntosh or Empire, peeled and cut into sixths

8 small prune plums, cut in halves and pitted

8 sprigs fresh thyme

Spaghetti Squash Salad

SERVES 6

THIS UNIQUE SALAD is one of my all-time favorites for a gathering. It lasts well on the table without wilting or losing quality as it sits. Most recently, I've been roasting the squash in the bonfire embers to add another layer of smoky complexity to its flavor. However, the salad works just as well if you roast the squash in the oven or even steam it.

FOR THE SQUASH

1 medium spaghetti squash

1 cup (340 g) julienned sun-dried tomatoes

3 green onions, sliced on the bias

¾ cup (40 g) Italian parsley or basil (30 g), julienned (fennel fronds, borage, or celery leaves also work well)

FOR THE DRESSING

¼ cup (65 ml) apple cider vinegar

⅓ cup (85 ml) extra-virgin olive oil, plus more if roasting squash

1 teaspoon Dijon mustard

1 clove garlic, crushed

1 teaspoon fine sea salt

1 teaspoon white pepper

Pinch of nutmeg

1. **COOK THE SQUASH.** If you are cooking over a live fire, keep the squash off to the edge of the fire in the embers. As it cooks, the skin will begin to blister and burn. Once you feel the squash give to mild pressure, it's ready to be removed from the fire. Let the squash rest and cool in a covered bowl, as it will continue to cook. If you're roasting the squash in the oven, cut it in half along the equator, scoop out the seeds and pulp, and add a few ounces of olive oil into the interior of the squash. Stand the squash on end in a roasting dish so the fats you added stay inside. Add a cup or so of water, cover the roasting dish with a lid or foil, and cook at 375°F (190°C) until soft. Set aside to cool.

2. Once the squash has cooled, use a fork to scrape out the flesh into a large mixing bowl. Try to keep the strands as long as possible, as it adds to the visual appeal of the dish.

3. Add the tomatoes, onions, and herbs to the mixing bowl.

4. **MAKE THE DRESSING.** Add the vinegar, oil, mustard, and garlic to a lidded jar. Shake vigorously to make a simple vinaigrette. Taste the dressing and add the salt, white pepper, and nutmeg to your preference.

5. Pour about half the dressing over the salad and toss gently so as not to break up the squash too much. There is more than enough dressing, so feel free to add more as desired.

Eggplant and Parsley Salad

SERVES 6

THIS IS A dish of contrasts. The bitterness of the parsley, the sweetness of the lightly roasted pepper, the tang and nuttiness of the dressing, and the soft meatiness of the eggplant and sun-dried tomatoes all play off each other to create a wondrously harmonious salad.

1. Cut the eggplant into 2-inch wedges. Liberally sprinkle the eggplant with the sea salt and place in a colander in the sink. Allow the eggplant to weep for about 30 minutes. Wipe off the extra salt with a wet paper towel.

2. Preheat the oven to 400°F (204°C). Place the eggplant on a baking sheet. Lightly brush the pieces with olive oil and sprinkle with pepper and garlic powder.

3. Roast the eggplant in the oven until it just softens, about 15 minutes. Cut the eggplant wedges into 2-inch squares.

4. Blacken the red bell pepper by placing it directly on a gas burner set on medium to medium-high heat. Char the skin on all sides. We want a crisp pepper without skin for the dish, so don't let the pepper cook on the burner. If you have an electric stove, use the oven broiler to char the skin, turning it as it chars. Once the pepper is fully blackened, place it in a ziplock bag—sweating it will help pull the skin from the pepper. When cool, wipe off the skin.

5. Cut the pepper in half pole to pole and remove the seeds, ribs, and stem. Dice the pepper into 1½-inch cubes.

6. In a large bowl, toss together the eggplant, parsley, sun-dried tomatoes, caraway seeds, and pepper cubes.

7. Whisk together the remainder of the olive oil, sesame oil, and vinegar to make a dressing. Toss the salad with the dressing and serve.

1 Italian or small globe eggplant

¼ cup (64 g) coarse sea salt

½ cup (125 ml) olive oil

1 tablespoon white pepper

1 tablespoon garlic powder

1 large red bell pepper

1 cup (50 g) Italian parsley leaves

½ cup (30 g) sun-dried tomatoes, sliced

1 tablespoon caraway seeds

1 teaspoon sesame oil

¼ cup (65 ml) sherry vinegar

Baby Kale and Fennel Salad

SERVES 6

I WENT TO grade school in the South, on the eastern shore of Maryland. Lunch at my elementary school included kale that was chopped and slow-cooked with fatback for hours. There weren't many third graders who liked slow-cooked kale, but there was one: me. In fact, I liked it so much that I traded other parts of my lunch to my friends so I could get their kale, too. I literally ate heaps of it, so much, in fact, that my school principal once called my mother to warn her against giving me any more greens that night with my supper.

To this day, raw or quick sautéed kale is not my thing, but give it to me slow-cooked with ham hocks and grits, and I'll stun you with how much I can eat. Baby kale though is a whole other thing. It's fresh and tender, superb in a salad, and holds up great to dressings. What's not to love?

1. Soak the raisins in the orange juice until softened, about 20 minutes.

2. Mix together all the dressing ingredients except for the olive oil. Drizzle the olive oil into the mixture slowly as you whisk to help emulsify the dressing. Set aside.

3. Strain the raisins. They should be plump but not soaking wet.

4. Mix all the salad ingredients together and dress lightly. There will be extra dressing, so feel free to add more as desired or reserve for a separate use.

USE WHAT YOU HAVE The extra salad dressing makes a tangy basting liquid for roasted chicken.

FOR THE DRESSING

½ cup (125 ml) whole milk yogurt

1 teaspoon ground cumin

1 tablespoon finely julienned preserved lemon peel (purchased or homemade, page 102)

1 teaspoon ground cinnamon

2 tablespoons apple cider vinegar

1 teaspoon fine sea salt

1 teaspoon white pepper

¼ cup (65 ml) extra-virgin olive oil

FOR THE SALAD

¼ cup (35 g) golden sultana raisins

½ cup (125 ml) fresh orange juice

6 ounces baby kale

4 tablespoons sliced raw almonds, toasted

1 tablespoon pumpkin seeds, toasted

½ medium bulb fresh fennel, shaved

¼ cup (35 g) currants

Warm Endive and Artichoke Salad

SERVES 4-6

IT'S UNDISPUTED THAT artichokes are difficult things to prepare—the process is time-consuming, knife-dulling, and finger-staining. It's equally undisputed, however, that they are worth every tribulation. Their brilliant floral flavor, dense meaty texture, and endless versatility are in all ways beautiful.

1. Add the flour to a large bowl and season with the salt and pepper. Whisk to combine and set aside.

2. **PREPARE THE ARTICHOKES.** Snap off the tough outside leaves around each of the artichokes until you get to the leaves that contain a small amount of the artichoke meat on the bottom. Then cut off the top of the artichoke until you see the very light green, almost white, part of the leaves, about 1–2 inches. Peel the outside of the stems with a peeler to remove the fibrous exterior. Cut the peeled artichokes in half.

3. With a spoon, dig out the choke (the hairy center leaves), but keep the pointy, soft, delicate interior leaves. Slice the artichokes from top to bottom, leaving the stems attached to as many slices as possible. Place the slices in a bowl of cold water with a few squeezes of lemon to keep them from browning.

4. **PREPARE AND COOK THE REMAINING VEGETABLES.** Rinse, dry, and tear the curly endive into bite-size pieces. Place in a bowl and set aside.

5. Toss the tomatoes in some of the olive oil and season with salt and cracked pepper. Place the tomatoes on one half of a baking sheet and the mushrooms on the other half and place under the broiler. Cook until slightly charred and blistered, about 2 minutes. If the mushrooms toast quicker than the tomatoes, remove them to a plate with a spatula and continue cooking the tomatoes until ready. Set aside.

6. **COOK THE ARTICHOKES.** Add about an inch of oil to a heavy-bottomed frying pan. Heat the oil over medium-high heat until it shimmers, just about smoking.

7. Remove the artichokes from the water and pat dry. Dredge in the seasoned flour, then place in the hot oil and cook until brown and tender. Remove to a paper towel and keep warm in a 200°F (93°C) oven until ready to serve.

8. Remove the pan from the heat and let the oil cool slightly. Pour about ¼ cup of the oil through a strainer into a bowl and discard the rest. Do not wipe out the pan.

9. **MAKE THE DRESSING.** Using the same pan (with its remaining light coating of oil), quickly sauté the capers and garlic. Add the strained oil to the pan and whisk in the juice of one lemon. Season with salt, pepper, and the fresh thyme.

10. Add the hot dressing to the bowl with the endive and toss to help wilt the lettuce. Finish the salad with the artichokes, tomatoes, and mushrooms.

---

1 cup (125 g) all-purpose flour

2 teaspoons kosher salt

2 teaspoons white pepper

2 fresh large globe artichokes with stems

1 pint of water (to cover)

2 lemons, juiced

1 small head curly endive

1 pint cherry or grape tomatoes

2 cups (500 ml) olive oil

Kosher salt and cracked pepper, to taste

1½ cups (82.5 g) oyster mushrooms

2 tablespoons capers

2 cloves garlic, crushed

1 tablespoon picked fresh thyme leaves

CHAPTER FIVE

NIGHT

REALIZATION.   REFLECTION.   UNFOLDING.

ONCE YOU'VE WRITTEN your home's story by designing a space that allows you to live your best life, you'll cherish your home and have the comfort and joy of sharing it with friends and family. Just like there are cycles to the day and to the seasons, design is ever evolving and unfolding. As are you. At Foxfire, we love to stay outside and witness the slow waning of the day as night comes on, that simple pleasure. The day is done, the work is done. The body and mind ease into rest as the day eases into night. We watch the shadows deepen and blur into the edge of the woods while the mountains turn an ever-darkening blue and the frog song rises with the moon. Fireflies light up the garden like a thousand tiny stars.

It's a time for reflection, looking back at where you've come from and looking ahead to where you're going. Too often, all the emphasis is put on the process and the project's completion, but it's important to revel for a while in what you've created. When you renovate or change a space, every decision you make about the decor is also about how you are deciding to live your life, creating a character for your home and the people who will enjoy it. The whole time we worked to create Foxfire, we were always thinking of the people who would come to stay, eat, and sleep on the property. Their overall experience was the priority, just as it is when creating a personal home. It needs to provide you comfort, rest, inspiration, and be a special haven. It must satisfy all your senses and touch your heart. ○

Continuing to Unfold

DECORATION EVOLVES WITH the passing of time, shifting tastes, and uses. Change your mind, play around. Let yourself go through phases of loving shells or the color pink or collecting old glass bottles. Your wardrobe changes over months and years, and so too should your living space evolve with current fashions and your own tastes. It seems just when I think I love a space and never want to change it, I change it.

In part, my abiding fondness for old cabinets comes from this desire to collect but also to keep swapping pieces out so spaces don't get stale or lose their mojo. The cabinets let me store items I still want to hold on to but don't necessarily want to showcase in a room at the moment. Poking through the cabinets every few months, I'll bring something out into the room and put another thing away until another time. Our philosophy of "use what you have" works perfectly for this since you can almost forget what you have stored in the cabinet (or closet, or basement), until a little further on down the road when you spy it suddenly with new eyes and find a great new setting for it. Decorating with your own stuff is the best and definitely cheaper than shopping in stores.

We're also constantly moving outside things inside, and everything in general all around. It gives the immediate gratification of a fresh look without the need to buy more stuff. Use what you have and let it transform and evolve. In the gardens, we use urns and planters to allow for the flexibility of changing plants or moving the pots around if we're having events and want certain flowers or colors to have more visibility and impact.

When moving things around to different rooms and "shopping" from our cabinets leaves us with items we're no longer excited about, sometimes, many times, we recycle through yard sales, give items away, or donate to Goodwill. The goal is never to clutter or bring in so many pieces that nothing stands out from the rest. Items need space, just as people do. With recycling, everything gets a second chance, and we love to see where our things end up next and how they're used in other people's homes once they've moved on to a future life.

We also regularly host Catskills swap parties where a few friends will come over and bring two or three knickknacks or small furnishings with them, like table lamps, artwork, or pillows. We pile everything on a table, pour glasses of wine, and draw numbers for the order in which we'll take turns choosing our new treasures. I got one of my favorite blue pitchers this way. The truth is that not every item gets picked up, but that justifies to the owner that they were probably right to get rid of it. Our rule is that once you've taken your old item out of your house, it can't go back in. The person who drew the number to choose first has the responsibility of taking any leftover items away to donate to the local charity thrift store.

Part of the process of reflection and letting your design unfold and evolve over time is to consider what you would do differently based on mistakes made and lessons learned. Sometimes the items that I end up bringing to our swap parties or donating to charity are because I bought them too soon. Often, the scale is off because I bought something before I had a handle on the actual finished dimensions of the room, or the color was blatantly wrong. We've done our humble best to take note of our design missteps so that we get it right the next time. ○

FROM THE DESK OF THE

FOXFIRE MOUNTAIN HOUSE

CATSKILL   MOUNTAINS

NEW YORK

It's about time for a
CATSKILLS SWAP!

Bring your favorite castaway smalls to swap with your kin folk.
Wine and snacks liberally provided.

LOCATION: Foxfire
DATE: December 6, 2018
TIME: 7-10pm

Luxury isn't about richness and money spent, but is the richness of simple indulgences and the magic of little unexpected things, like coming inside for the night with hair and clothes still carrying the musky woodsmoke scent of the bonfire. The dinner party has ended and guests have left the table. The wax has dripped down from the candles, and the cloth is rumpled and kissed with red-wine stains. That look of the table after a dinner gathering is, to me, at least as beautiful as the freshly set table before guests arrive.

(opposite) A perfect home isn't possible, but when care is shown with thoughtful details, personality shines through, and that's what makes a place feel homey.

(above) It's amazing the satisfaction that comes from having things around you that you connect with and simply enjoy looking at—knickknacks and mementos with meaning. In a way, that's the basis of home to me, almost as much as seeing our dog asleep in a sunny spot on the sofa.

(right) We knew our guests would sit in front of the blazing fireplace in the lounge at night before heading upstairs to bed, and so we wanted to make those end-of-day reflective moments extra special. We decided to get a fireback that would rest against the rear wall of the hearth behind the flames. Cast-iron firebacks have traditionally been used to radiate even more heat into the room, but they also have a beautiful sculptural effect that provides another layer to view along with the fire. When I came across a fox design, I knew it was perfect, not only for the play on "Foxfire," but because it was a lovely ode to our goal of honoring the wildlife of our space that I thought would be memorable for our guests.

| DIY | Foxfire Dream Tea Blend | MAKES 1 SERVING |

THIS IS A comforting nighttime tea to soothe you when you're worked up or just to help you relax. We blend it ourselves from herbs we find on our property, and it encourages the best sleep. We love its subtle lavender undercurrents and delicate wild chamomile top notes. Sweet dreams are guaranteed.

INGREDIENTS

4 parts wild thyme

2 parts young spring spruce needles (the lighter-colored younger shoots will be sweeter and more lemony, and darker older shoots will be more tangy and strong-tasting, but also contain more flavonoids and vitamin C), chopped finely

6 parts wild chamomile, chopped finely

1 part lavender buds, chopped finely

2 parts lemongrass, chopped finely

1. Strip the flowers and leaves from the thyme sprigs and discard the stems.

2. Spread the herbs out on a sheet tray and let dry for a day or two, moving them gently now and then for air circulation.

3. Blend all the dried herbs together using a mortar and pestle.

4. To serve, place 1 tablespoon of the blend in a sachet and steep in 1 cup of boiled water. Sweeten with honey, if desired. **o**

Reflections

MANY OF THE decisions we've made are based on our own impulses and intuition, like trying to lock in a vision from a dream you can't fully remember, or a distant childhood memory. Movies we've seen that have stayed with us, our travels and wanderings, passions like our love of the natural world—all the experiences of our lives have gone into the design and decorating of Foxfire. It has been a quest to marry those personal moments with the rigors of hard work and learning to run a small business as creative entrepreneurs. This is why we're never worried about competition and support the growth of all the businesses around us in our local community and beyond. By the nature of it, we all do things differently and that's to be celebrated.

Nothing has made us prouder than saving and transforming this once dilapidated old building and contributing to the preservation of a piece of Catskills history. As Foxfire transformed, so did we. We've learned a lot about so many things (not the least of which our handyman skills have increased tenfold, that's for sure). Thank you, Pinterest, for so much inspiration and letting us organize our ideas into visual boards for easy reference and sharing. Thank you, Craigslist and YouTube, we couldn't have done it without you. Most recently, we've been taking on design projects for clients. Buying a house in New York City is out of reach for so many people now with real estate prices sky-high, and so we're excited to see more and more properties in the country becoming people's first homes. Some continue to live and work in the city during the week and come upstate on weekends, and some have made the transition to full-time country life. We've loved being asked to bring our Foxfire aesthetic to the design and renovation of their new homes. Many properties are also going to be rented as Airbnbs, and we've enjoyed sharing our hospitality tips. More than anything, we've loved that people aren't waiting to have the lifestyle they want, they're making it happen.

We hope this book might inspire you to take risks, to write the story of your home so you can design a place where your senses are awakened, your heart and soul are full, and you live life as your best self. Join us on the brink where everything is possible. Dreamers like us always meet here, and you see—the view is wildly beautiful. ○

RECITES

ONE OF THE things that always strikes me about hosting, and hospitality especially, is that there's a rush of behind-the-scenes preparation before guests arrive, but once they do, all is gracious serenity. Everything slows right down to the things that really matter, like warm greetings, conversation and stories shared, hearty food heaped on plates. This is where the art of slow living and the pleasure of cooking slowly while guests wind down, rest, reflect, and dream come together in the most beautiful union.

Overnight Olive and Rosemary Focaccia

**MAKES
2 LOAVES**

THIS IS OUR signature bread at Foxfire that we serve with all the meals in the restaurant. It's best started before you go to bed so that you'll have it ready for the next night's dinner. I love slow fermentation of doughs. It adds remarkable depth of flavor. This is a very simple recipe, with no kneading required. It isn't exactly like traditional focaccias in that it's a little denser and chewier, but it perfectly retains the taste and lusciousness of the olive oil. The use of a cast-iron skillet helps hold the oil so it absorbs as it cooks and gives a great crust to the bread. This focaccia freezes really well, so the recipe is enough to make two loaves. You'll find it goes fast!

9 cups (1.13 kg) bread flour

1 tablespoon fine sea salt

1½ teaspoons active dry yeast

3 cups (750 ml) very warm water

1 cup (250 ml) olive oil

1 cup (142 g) oil-cured olives

2 sprigs rosemary leaves

2 tablespoons coarse sea salt

1. Add the flour to a medium-size mixing bowl and whisk in the fine sea salt.

2. Put the yeast in a large mixing bowl, add the warm water, and stir gently. Immediately pour in the flour mixture and mix the dough with a rubber spatula until all dry bits are incorporated. Cover tightly with plastic wrap and let rise in a warm place for at least 18 hours.

3. Lightly dust the proofed dough with flour and dump it out of the bowl onto a clean counter or pastry board. Divide into two parts.

4. Add ¼ cup of the olive oil to each of two 10-inch cast-iron skillets. Place one part of the dough in each of the skillets.

5. Drizzle about 3 tablespoons of oil on the top of each dough and cover lightly with plastic wrap. Place in a warm spot until the doughs have doubled in size.

6. Preheat the oven to 500°F (260°C). Press half of the olives into each dough and sprinkle on the rosemary leaves. Pour half of the remaining olive oil over each, and sprinkle with coarse sea salt.

7. Bake for 15 minutes or until golden brown.

Mussel Soup

SERVES 4

THERE WERE A few influential cookbooks in my youth. The first was the *Woman's Day Encyclopedia of Cooking*, which is how I learned to read sitting on my mother's lap. Then Jacques Pépin's *La Technique*, the unabridged edition of Escoffier's master work, and the Time Life series *The Good Cook*. I would pore over these for hours and then venture into the kitchen to try out new methods.

One of the techniques that I read about in the Time Life series on soups was using eggs as a thickening agent. The results were sublime—it gave the soups a velvety texture and a creamy, elegant finish. Best of all, it wasn't that easy to do, so it went straight into my bag of tricks to impress.

In the end, it's not that the method is that hard, you just need to be sure to temper the eggs at the start by adding some of the hot soup liquid to them, which allows you to bring up their temperature gradually without scrambling them before adding them to the soup stock. Once you get this technique down, you can make incredibly refined soups and sauces.

1. Clean the mussels. If you bought farm-raised, they'll be pretty clean as far as beards are concerned, but wild mussels will need to be checked closely. The beard is the attachment the mollusk uses to hold on to whatever it lives on and that isn't a good thing to eat, so it needs to be pulled off.

2. Heat a medium saucepan with a lid over high heat. When the pan is hot, drop in the cleaned mussels. Stir the mussels in the pan and bring the pan back to full heat.

3. Pour in the wine and sherry and cover immediately to catch the steam. Cook the mussels for about 3 minutes, or until they just open. Remove them from the heat. Strain the wine and liquid from the pot and reserve.

4. Pull the mussels from the shells and discard the shells. If any are very large, cut them in half—you want them to fit easily on a soup spoon. Set the mussel meat aside.

5. In a large, clean saucepan over medium-low heat, melt 4 tablespoons of the butter, and add the shallots and the garlic. Sweat until soft but not brown.

6. Add in the mussel meat, reserved liquid from step 3, and the milk. Stir to combine and bring to a simmer. Do not boil or scald the milk.

7. Place the 4 egg yolks in a mixing bowl. Remove about 1½ cups of the hot liquid from the pan, and very slowly whisk it into the eggs to temper them. (It starts the emulsification process to prevent the proteins from coagulating.)

8. Turn the heat down to medium low and whisk the egg mixture into the soup.

9. Stir constantly as the soup thickens. Once the soup has thickened enough that it coats the back of a spoon, remove it from the heat. Whisk in the remaining 2 tablespoons of butter. This will give the soup a nice gloss and finish.

10. Gently stir in the chives and chervil, and add salt, pepper, and nutmeg to taste. Serve.

1 pound fresh mussels

1 cup (250 ml) dry white wine

1 ounce dry sherry

3 thyme sprigs

⅜ cup (170 g) sweet butter

½ shallot, finely diced

2 cloves garlic, finely diced

1 quart (946 ml) whole milk

4 egg yolks

1 tablespoon chopped chives

1 tablespoon torn fresh chervil leaves

1 teaspoon fine sea salt

1 teaspoon white pepper

Pinch of nutmeg

Slow-Cooked Basque Country Pork Ribs

SERVES 4

I DISCOVERED THIS dish when one of our Foxfire wedding couples wanted a Spanish-themed wedding feast. The Basque elements such as the smoked paprika, olives, and spices fit in perfectly with our culinary repertoire. I love slow-cooking meat, and you can't beat pork ribs with fatty, meaty loins and bones attached. It's both economical and delicious at the same time.

1. Place the pork into a large bowl and add ½ cup salt, sugar, warm water, bay leaves, and cloves. Stir to incorporate, and let the meat marinate for at least half an hour. This is a great extra step that adds flavor and moisture to the meat and can be done while prepping the rest of the dish.

2. In a large oven-safe pan, heat a tablespoon of olive oil over medium-high heat, and quickly brown the onion, pepper, olives, and garlic; they should still have a firm texture. Remove the vegetables from the pan and set aside. Wipe out any excess browned bits at the bottom of the pan.

3. Preheat the oven to 300°F (149°C). Remove the pork from the marinade and pat dry. Add an additional tablespoon of oil and heat over medium-high heat. Add the pork and sauté until browned on all sides.

4. Remove the pork and set aside. Deglaze the pan by adding the red wine and scraping up the browned bits from the bottom.

5. Return everything to the pan and stir in the smoked paprika, carrots, and crushed tomatoes.

6. Transfer the pan to the oven and cook for 45 minutes. The pork is done when it is tender and pulls easily from the bone but does not fall apart when you lift it from the pan. Transfer the pork and vegetables to a warm serving dish.

7. Place the cherry tomatoes on a sheet pan and season with ½ teaspoon of salt. Turn the oven to the broil setting, and broil the tomatoes until charred. Watch the tomatoes closely; this process takes only a few minutes.

8. Garnish the pork with parsley and the charred cherry tomatoes and serve.

USE WHAT YOU HAVE The leftovers for this dish make a perfect burrito lunch. Add some rice, beans, and feta or cotija cheese to a flour tortilla and top with the warmed-up ribs and sauce. So good.

---

3 pounds country pork ribs

½ cup (124 g) plus ½ teaspoon kosher salt

½ cup (110 g) brown sugar

2 quarts warm water

3 bay leaves

6 whole cloves

2 tablespoons olive oil

1 medium yellow onion, coarsely chopped

1 red bell pepper, finely diced

¼ cup (40 g) pitted kalamata olives

3 cloves garlic, minced

¾ cup (190 ml) rioja (or other red wine)

1 teaspoon smoked paprika

1½ medium carrots, peeled and diced

1 cup (225 g) crushed tomatoes

1 pint cherry tomatoes

¼ cup (13 g) fresh parsley leaves

Our favorite dessert for a gathering is toasted marshmallows over the bonfire because it's the Catskills, and, honestly, nothing tastes better. Sharing wonderful meals outdoors with friends, talking and laughing long into the evening, is the essence of a good life.

Fig and Goat Yogurt Galette

SERVES 6

I OFTEN SPEAK about simplicity coming with experience, and this dish is a perfect example of that. There was a time when I would have made this as a tart with a lot of fancy steps—a blind baked shortbread crust, crème patisserie as the base, and the fruit would have been arranged in a spiral then finished with an apricot glaze. A very nice dish, but fussy. This is a simpler, more rustic version, so in a way, it's both a more modern take and a much older style at the same time.

1. **MAKE THE CRUST.** Place the flours, salt, and sugars in a food processor. Pulse the machine to mix the ingredients.

2. Drop the cold butter into the machine piece by piece while pulsing. Take it a little at a time—you want to cut the butter into the flour until it achieves the texture of wet sand. If you run it too long, that will soften the butter and make a paste.

3. Transfer the mixture to a mixing bowl and add a little water at a time to bring the dough together. Knead lightly. Once formed into a ball that will hold together, stop working it. The less you work the dough, the better and flakier the crust will be.

4. Wrap the dough in plastic wrap and chill in the fridge for at least an hour.

5. **MAKE THE FILLING.** Quarter the figs and then cut the persimmons to match. Toss the fruit in the sugar in a bowl and let it sit to macerate for an hour or more at room temperature.

6. In a separate bowl, fold the goat yogurt, egg yolks, and honey together. Keep the mixture as firm as possible. Set aside.

7. **ASSEMBLE THE GALETTE.** Preheat the oven to 400°F (204°C). Remove the dough from the fridge. On a well-floured pastry board, roll the dough out to about 8 x 14 inches. Transfer the dough to a parchment-lined or floured and buttered baking sheet.

8. Gently place the yogurt mixture in the center of the dough, leaving about 1½ inches around the edges. Use a slotted spoon to place three-quarters of the fruit over the yogurt. You want to avoid transferring too much liquid from the fruit.

9. Fold the edges up and around the fruit and pinch the seams closed. Top the galette with the remainder of the fruit.

10. In a small bowl, whisk the extra egg and use a pastry brush to brush it over the exposed crust. Sprinkle the galette with the extra turbinado sugar.

11. Bake for about 25 minutes, until the pastry is done and the juices from the fruit have started to thicken. Remove and let cool. Before serving, glaze the fruit with the reserved honey.

FOR THE CRUST

1¼ (155 g) cups all-purpose flour, plus more for dusting

¼ cup (30 g) whole wheat flour

½ teaspoon salt

1 tablespoon granulated cane sugar

1 tablespoon turbinado or light brown sugar

½ cup (113 g) cold unsalted butter, cut into ½-inch cubes

4 tablespoons cold water (adjust as needed)

FOR THE FILLING

3 medium-size fresh figs

1 medium-size mostly ripe persimmon (see Note)

½ cup (100 g) granulated cane sugar

1 cup (250 ml) Greek-style goat milk yogurt

2 egg yolks

½ cup (125 ml) honey, reserve ¼ cup for glazing

FOR THE TOPPING

1 large whole egg

¼ cup (50 g) turbinado sugar

NOTE: A fully ripe persimmon is very soft, super sweet, and juicy. An unripe one is stone hard and very tannic. For this recipe, we want one that's sweet but semi-firm.

Wild Blackberry Coffee Cake

SERVES 6

AS A CHEF, I became a night owl by necessity, not by choice. So whenever possible, I choose to make breakfast for our guests, prep for the dinner menu, and take us through the bulk of the evening service before leaving the rest of the night to my team. There's a real joy to rising early and having a quiet, clean kitchen to work in before our guests get up and come to the dining room for breakfast. We have a large wild blackberry patch growing behind the glass house and as long as I can get to it before the birds do, I can fill my basket with the fruit. There's nothing I like better than putting on the coffee, walking outside through the morning dew to the gardens, and gathering berries and herbs fresh from nature to serve on our table. This is a favorite cake of ours because it's as satisfying to wake up to as it is to have after dinner.

1. Preheat the oven to 350°F (177°C). Butter and flour a Bundt pan.

2. **MAKE THE CAKE.** Sift the flour, baking powder, and one teaspoon of the salt together in a small bowl.

3. Combine the yogurt, milk, vanilla, and lemon zest.

4. In a stand mixer set to medium high, cream the butter, the sugars, and the remaining teaspoon of salt together until light and airy.

5. Pour the eggs into the butter mixture and mix until just combined. Incorporate the flour and milk mixtures a little at a time, alternating between each until just combined.

6. **MAKE THE TOPPING.** In a separate bowl, mix together the topping ingredients.

7. **ASSEMBLE AND BAKE THE CAKE.** Add ¼ of the batter to the Bundt pan, then add half the blackberries, half the remaining batter, the remaining blackberries, then finish off with the last quarter of the batter.

8. Place the cake in the oven. When the cake is three-quarters baked, about 35 minutes, open the oven and sprinkle the topping over the cake.

9. Finish cooking the cake until a skewer pulls out clean, about 8 to 10 more minutes.

10. Remove and cool the cake in the pan. When it's cool enough to handle, invert it out of the pan, turn the cake back right side up, and serve warm.

FOR THE CAKE

4 cups (500 g) flour

1 tablespoon baking powder

2 teaspoons fine sea salt

1 cup (250 ml) whole-milk yogurt

1 cup (250 ml) whole milk

2 teaspoons vanilla extract

Zest of ½ lemon

1 cup (225 g) unsalted butter, softened to room temperature

2½ cups (500 g) granulated cane sugar

½ cup (110 g) brown sugar

3 eggs, whisked

1 pint blackberries

FOR THE TOPPING

¼ cup (20 g) old-fashioned rolled oats

1 tablespoon cinnamon

¼ cup (30 g) all-purpose flour

¼ cup (57 g) unsalted butter, melted

Black Pepper Strawberries and Cream

SERVES 4

SHORTLY AFTER I finished high school, I picked up a job at a posh continental-style restaurant that had just opened on the ground floor of a newly constructed office tower. The restaurant had waiters in tuxedos, several gueridon servers for making tableside Caesar salads and flaming desserts—old-school fine dining. Looking around New York City today, it seems that the classics are coming back. This is one of my favorite old-school desserts that I think is ready to be in the limelight again.

1. Add the cream, lemon juice, and yogurt to a mason jar, cover with a cloth, and leave in a warm place for 12 hours or until thick. This will become your crème fraîche topping.

2. One hour before serving, combine the strawberries, figs, pastis, three-quarters of the sugar, and lemon zest in a serving bowl.

3. Right before serving, crack the black pepper over top and sprinkle with the remaining sugar. Crown with a dollop of the crème fraîche.

1 cup (250 ml) heavy cream

Juice of ½ lemon

1 tablespoon whole-milk yogurt

1 pint strawberries, hulled, some whole and others sliced to a consistent size

3 fresh figs, quartered

2 ounces pastis

¼ cup (50 g) granulated cane sugar

Zest of 1 lemon

Coarse cracked black pepper

Lime-Infused Pound Cake

MAKES 1 LOAF

THIS IS MY chef version of my favorite birthday cake from when I was a child. My mother made this cake from a box mix, with lime Jell-O and limeade. Although my mother is a superb cook, this style of cake was very much of the time (plus she had a busy career and five of us kids, so no judgment). I loved the way the tart icing absorbed into the dense buttery cake to make a doughnut-like texture, almost like those sweet packaged treats from the corner store. But what I didn't like, even as a child, was the artificial taste and the fact that the stuff never went bad. That's just not normal. So I created this version with all the flavor and texture but none of the additives.

1. **MAKE THE CAKE.** Preheat the oven to 350°F (177°C). Butter and flour a 5 x 9-inch loaf pan and set aside. In a small bowl, sift together the flour, baking powder, and salt.

2. In the bowl of a stand mixer, cream the butter and sugar together until light and fluffy. Add the vanilla, then mix in the eggs and milk. Gradually add the flour mix into the wet ingredients, mixing until just combined each time.

3. Pour the batter into the prepared pan. Bake for 50 minutes, or until a skewer pulls out cleanly. Remove from the oven and let cool for 5 minutes to set the crust.

4. **MAKE THE GLAZE.** Mix together all the glaze ingredients to a slurry-like consistency.

5. Poke many holes throughout the top of the cake with a fork. Pour all the glaze gradually over the cake and let it seep in. Chill the cake for at least 15 minutes until the glaze is set.

6. **MAKE THE MILK FROSTING.** Mix the milk, salt, and flour together in a saucepan. Heat over medium-high heat until boiling. Boil the mixture slowly for one minute.

7. Remove from heat, cover with plastic wrap, and let stand until it comes to room temperature. Then place the mixture in the fridge and chill thoroughly.

8. In the bowl of a stand mixer, cream the butter and sugar together until light and fluffy. Add the vanilla.

9. Turn the mixer speed to low and slowly blend in the chilled milk mixture. Mix for about 3 minutes. The finished result should be reminiscent of cream cheese icing.

10. Serve the pound cake sliced with a dollop of milk frosting on the side.

FOR THE CAKE

1½ cups (190 g) all-purpose flour

1 teaspoon baking powder

¼ teaspoon salt

1 cup (225 g) unsalted butter, softened to room temperature

¾ cup (150 g) granulated cane sugar

1½ teaspoons pure vanilla extract

3 large eggs, whisked, at room temperature

3 tablespoons milk, at room temperature

FOR THE GLAZE

1 cup (250 ml) fresh lime juice

1½ cups (190 g) confectioners' sugar

Zest of 2 limes

FOR THE MILK FROSTING

2 cups (500 ml) whole milk

½ teaspoon table salt

¼ cup (30 g) all-purpose flour

2 cups (450 g) unsalted butter, softened to room temperature

2 cups (400 g) granulated cane sugar

1 tablespoon vanilla extract

RESOURCES

BRANDING DESIGN

LAND
workbyland.com

BEDDING

Parachute Home
parachutehome.com

BATH PRODUCTS

Hudson Naturals
hudson-naturals.com

CANDLES

Cavern New York
cavernnewyork.com

WALLPAPER

Lake August
lakeaugust.com

CUSTOM STITCHING

Fort Lonesome
ftlonesome.com

FLEA MARKETS

Brimfield
brimfieldantiquefleamarket.com

Madison-Bouckville
madison-bouckville.com

ANTIQUES

Canvas House Antiques
canvashouseantiques.blogspot.com

Habitat for Humanity Restores
habitat.org/restores

Hudson Antiques Warehouse
cottagetreasuresonline.com

Hudson Valley House Parts
hvhouseparts.com

Newburgh Vintage Emporium
newburghvintageemporium.com

Point Pleasant Antique Emporium
pointpleasantantiques.com

Red Chair on Warren
redchair-antiques.com

Rhinebeck Antique Emporium
rhinebeckantiqueemporium.com

Zaborski Emporium
stanthejunkman.com

GARDEN CENTERS

Adams Fairacre Farms
adamsfarms.com

Augustine Nursery
augustinenursery.com

Gallo's of Woodstock
2542 Route 212, Woodstock, NY

FARMERS AND FOOD PRODUCERS

Beaverkill Trout Hatchery
beaverkill-trout-hatchery.business.site

Catsmo Artisan Smokehouse
catsmo.com

Chaseholm Farm
chaseholmfarm.com

Churchtown Dairy
churchtowndairy.org

Common Ground Farm
commongroundfarm.org

Common Hands Farm
commonhandscsa.com

Farms2Tables
farms2tables.com

Hawthorne Valley Creamery
farm.hawthornevalley.org

Heermance Farm
heermancefarm.com

Hepworth Farms
hepworthfarms.com

Jacuterie
jacuterie.com

Lenny B's Smoked Trout
403 Wittenberg Rd., Bearsville NY

Miracle Springs Farm
miraclespringsfarm.com

Obercreek Farm
obercreekfarm.com

Ronnybrook Farm Dairy
ronnybrook.com

Smoke House of the Catskills
724 Route 212, Saugerties, NY

Sparrowbush Farm
sparrowbushfarm.com

Sprout Creek Farm
sproutcreekfarm.org

Sun Sprout Farm
sunsproutfarm.com

Whistle Down Farm
whistledownfarm.com

Yellow Bell Farm
yellowbellfarm.net

BREWERS, CIDERIES, AND DISTILLERS

Arrowood Farm Brewery
arrowoodfarms.com

Berkshire Mountain Distillers
berkshiremountaindistillers.com

Catskill Brewery
catskillbrewery.com

Hillrock Distillery
hillrockdistillery.com

Metal House Cider
metalhousecider.com

Sloop Brewing Co.
sloopbrewing.com

West Kill Brewing
westkillbrewing.com

Woodstock Brewing
drinkwoodstock.com

ACKNOWLEDGMENTS

A WORLD OF thanks to everyone who has helped us make the dream of what Foxfire Mountain House could be a reality, and in the process, changed our lives as a family for the better (for the best). We are forever grateful.

So many talented people worked hard to build Foxfire with us, and we couldn't have done it without them all. Thank you all very much for sharing your crafts and skills along the way.

Our profound thanks to Rene Symonds for your enduring faith and integral support of the project(s) and for granting us your trust throughout. We will always thank our lucky stars for your involvement.

Emilie Sinkler, you are a wonder. Where would we ever be without your endless kindness, generosity, friendship, and savvy ways in the world? You enrich our Catskills life on every front.

Thank you to Land Boys for our beautiful branding that has done so much to tell the story of Foxfire from day one.

From the very early days, we have had the most incredible staff who devote their vibrant energy, creativity, and good hearts to making Foxfire a memorably hospitable and beautiful place for those who visit. We're so proud and truly thankful to each one of you, past, present, and future. Our amazing GM, Chris Sikora, isn't big on compliments, but it must be said that without your brilliant running of the ship, we'd never be able to dream about what's next.

Thank you to all the Catskills and Hudson Valley businesses that are our neighbors and colleagues. You inspire us daily and we're so excited to continue to grow with you.

To our beloved guests, thank you for coming to Foxfire to stay, to dine, to celebrate special occasions and life moments, to elope, to be wed, to retreat, to relax. Everything we do, everything we are is because of you. We are humbled and honored you continue to choose us.

Thank you to our publishing team at Harper Design, especially our editor, Cristina Garces, and designer, Amanda Jane Jones, for making this book more beautiful than we dared hope.

Thank you to Matt Cully, gifted musician. No one knows musicology like you! You bring the music to Foxfire through your ridiculously good playlists that we share monthly on Spotify.

To Diane Kochendorfer, Tim's mom, the start of it all and the deepest thank you of them all for being Tim's first and best teacher, and his biggest supporter. You will always be the grandest inspiration for how to live, love, and enjoy life. Many of the recipes in this book are directly based on the glories from your kitchen, and you are, and will continue to be, one of the greatest. We love you.

Thank you, readers, for being interested in our story—we hope it's been inspiring to you. And if your wanderings take you to the Catskills, come by and see us! You can follow along on our journeys on Instagram @foxfiremountainhouse.

ELIZA CLARK & TIM TROJIAN

FORMERLY A TELEVISION showrunner and writer, Eliza has had a lifelong passion for interior design, and is grateful that Foxfire Mountain House was the chance to tell a new kind of story. Eliza's designs for Foxfire have been featured in *Vogue*, *Domino*, *Elle*, Remodelista, Apartment Therapy, *House & Garden*, Goop, and *Condé Nast Traveler*, among others.

TIM HAS WORKED in kitchens since he was fifteen, and for the past several years has worked as an executive chef and food and beverage director. Fresh, seasonal, and locally produced with global influences from Korea to Sweden, Tim's dishes are inspired by the ingredients he finds. He secretly thrives on limitations and swears that many of his best dishes came from cleaning out the fridge.

ARDEN WRAY Arden is an award-winning photographer based in Toronto and New York. Her work has appeared in outlets including the *New York Times*, Urban Outfitters, and West Elm.